PRAISE FOR *Eas.*

"Lam describes our new Pacific world in prose that is subtle, mesmerizing, and unforgettable."—Jeff Chang, author of *Can't Stop Won't Stop: A History of the Hip-Hop Generation* and *Who We Be: The Colorization of America*

"Andrew Lam is an expert time-traveler, collapsing childhood and adulthood; years of war and peace; and the evolution of language in his own life, time, and mind. To read Andrew's work is a joy and a profound journey."—Farai Chideya, reporter and author of *Kiss the Sky*

"Lam's story is heartbreaking and inspiring as it tells of the travails, the tragedies, and the successes of the Vietnamese and other Asians who came to America to escape oppression and better their lives and the lives of their children and in the process, blessed and changed America."—Larry Engelmann, author of *Tears before the Rain: An Oral History of the Fall of South Vietnam*

"One of the best American essayists of his generation." —Wayne Karlin, author of *Wandering Souls: Journeys with the Dead and the Living in Viet Nam*

"By turns playful, thoughtful, and critically astute, this is his version of the voice the New America speaks, and it is a superbly fresh lyric. *East Eats West* is a sublime dissertation on what happens when the 'marginal' finally arrives at the 'center.'"—Rubén Martínez, Fletcher Jones Chair in Literature and Writing at Loyola Marymount University and author of *Crossing Over: A Mexican Family on the Migrant Trail*

"Andrew Lam's work weaves journalism and storytelling beautifully. Together the essays craft a new Vietnamese American identity that is invested in neither retrieving 'authentic' culture or claiming America. Lam's vision is shaped by the past, not beholden to it, and trusting of the future."—Isabelle Thuy Pelaud, associate professor of Asian American studies at San Francisco State University

"No one writes about being Vietnamese and American with a finer sadness or a richer sense of irony or greater humor than Andrew Lam." —Richard Rodriguez, author of *Brown: The Last Discovery of America*

"With a sharp eye on American idiosyncrasies, with a sad understanding of the inevitable distance between immigrant parents and their children, with a nuanced hopefulness for culinary utopias, and with an unstoppable curiosity to fathom the layered multilingual memories of an immigrant, *East Eats West* initiates the reader to the fact that 'in the land of plenty there's plenty of irony' too."—Werner Sollors, professor of African and African American studies, Harvard University, author of *Beyond Ethnicity: Consent and Descent in American Culture*

"Sometimes sweet, sometimes bitter, always delicious, Andrew Lam's elegantly plated and richly spiced morsels of transcultural observation are a must for anyone interested in delving deeper into the evolving social palate of a nation whose tastes, aspirations and desires are more shaped by immigrant influences than ever before. Indeed, given that the "melting pot" has long since been dismissed as a description of our diverse society, commentators might do well to look to Lam's musings on the quintessential dish of his heritage, pho, for a substitute metaphor—America as an interwoven tangle of discrete ingredients, each lending flavor to the others, and held together by a broth of infinite richness and depth that incorporates the best of each. *East Eats West* is a movable feast for a nouvelle America that, like all great meals, leaves you both fully satiated yet somehow hungry for more." —Jeff Yang, "Asian Pop" columnist for the *San Francisco Chronicle*

EAST EATS WEST
Writing in Two Hemispheres

ANDREW LAM

Heyday, Berkeley, California

"Who Will Light Incense?", "Mourning the Loss of the Tiger," "Singing in the Family," "In Search of Hermes' Belt," "Stress, Vietnamese-Style," "Too Much Self-Esteem Can Be Bad for Your Child," "Our Man Obama: The Post-Imperial Presidency," "Letter to a Young Iraqi Refugee to America," and "Can Ghosts Cross the Ocean?" first appeared in *New American Media* and are reproduced with permission.

"Wild, Wild East," "California Cuisine of the World" (originally "Diversity Feeds California Cuisine"), and "Letters from a Younger Brother" (originally "Letter to Myself") first appeared in *California Magazine*.

Library of Congress Cataloging-in-Publication Data
Lam, Andrew.
  East eats West : writing in two hemispheres / Andrew Lam.
    p. cm.
  ISBN 978-1-59714-138-3 (pbk. : alk. paper)
  1. Lam, Andrew. 2. Vietnamese Americans—Biography. 3. Vietnamese Americans—Social life and customs. 4. Culture diffusion—United States. 5. Culture diffusion—Vietnam. I. Title.
  E184.V53L358 2010
  973'.0495—dc22

                              2010017834

Cover Design: Lorraine Rath
Interior Design: Rebecca LeGates
Printing and Binding: Thomson-Shore, Dexter, MI

Orders, inquiries, and correspondence should be addressed to:
  Heyday
  P. O. Box 9145, Berkeley, CA 94709
  (510) 549-3564, Fax (510) 549-1889
  www.heydaybooks.com

10 9 8 7 6 5 4 3 2 1

CONTENTS

TO AMY, ERIC, AND BRANDON

ACKNOWLEDGMENTS

I have a few mentors to thank: Richard Rodriguez, for his kindness and wise counsel; Sandy Close, who provides an unconventional environment for a quirky writer; and her husband, Franz Schurmann, who was de facto my world politics and history professor for many years after I graduated from college. I am inspired by my good friend Milbert, who travels to some very hot spots for the sake of human rights.

I also am indebted to my mother, whose stories of Vietnam stay deep in her psyche even if the contemporary American landscape begins to fade, and of course my father, who, despite his own grief, shares much of his worldly wisdom with his children. And last, I am thankful to my first English teacher, Mr. Kaeselau, whose kindness will always stay deep in my heart.

INTRODUCTION

Whenever I hear the word *chua*, Vietnamese for "sour," I think
of tamarind, the sticky brown fruit that grew in abundance
on shading trees in my old schoolyard back in Saigon, and its
intense sour-sweet memories inevitably cause my molars to
vibrate and my mouth to water. I hear "sour" in English and I
don't feel a thing.

And yet, it is in English now that I ply my trade, it is in English that I dream and think, and it is in English that I best express
myself. Vietnam, its language, its memories, are reduced to a kind
of lullaby, which is to say, visceral and yet out of the quotidian of
my life.

Such are the strange bearings of those who lurk between East
and West, between languages, between memories and desires.
Where the two hemispheres overlap, however, is where I learned
and relearned how to mediate opposed ideas and to bridge disparate viewpoints. A barely charted territory, it is fraught with contradictions and tensions, its waters treacherous with the various
tugs and undercurrents.

Over the years I have watched the East and West pas de deux
as forces of history as well as my own fragmented biography.
The differences I learned very early on. In Vietnam you do not
look your teachers in the eye unless it is to challenge them. In
America if you fail to look your teachers in the eye they may
think you shifty, that you have something to hide. Americans are
fond of saying, "I love you." Vietnamese don't share words of

affection very easily, if at all. No, they show it; it's all in the gestures—working three jobs so your kids can go to private school, saving the best apple for your spouse while eating the bruised one yourself. Americans celebrate birthdays. Vietnamese light incense and have feasts on death anniversaries of important relatives. American children can't wait to leave home at eighteen, Vietnamese children stay around long into adulthood, and often even after they marry. In Vietnam individualism is equated with selfishness. America elevates it to an ideology, it demands it: life, liberty, and the pursuit of happiness. America whispers rebellion of the individual against the communal: Follow your dream.

Perhaps it is easier to abandon one system and swallow the new. Then perhaps life wouldn't be so difficult for those who migrate East to West. But the melting pot concept hasn't really worked. It is more like a blender into which differences are forced and then regurgitated as platitudes, sort of like Disney movies, which rewrite all complicated stories toward a single outcome, a thinning, predictable, happily-ever-after formula.

The modern condition, the reality, on the other hand, is messy, defined by mismatch and by an intensifying and growing complexity. Or rather, increasingly it is cosmopolitanism that is the norm. According to the French writer Pascal Bruckner, cosmopolitanism speaks of being rooted in the depths of several layers of memory, in numerous particularities. "It does not collect a trait here or there. It becomes incarnate. It means counterbalancing the land of one's birth with additional homelands." I think of it as something like Michael Ondaatje's novel *The English Patient,* in which a set of complicated characters with variant and divergent histories decide to populate an abandoned villa, and in it they argue and fall in love, and in between they tell each other their stories.

Here's mine. I grew up a patriotic South Vietnamese living in Vietnam during the war. I remember singing the national anthem, swearing my allegiance to the flag, and promising my soul and body to protect the land and its sacred rice fields and rivers. Wide-eyed child that I was, I believed every word.

But then the war ended and I, along with my family (and eventually a couple of million other Vietnamese), betrayed our agrarian ethos and land-bound sentiments by fleeing overseas to lead a very different life.

These days I regularly travel between East Asia and the United States as an American journalist and writer. My relatives, once all concentrated in Saigon, are scattered across three continents, speaking three and four other languages, becoming citizens of several different countries. Once communal and bound by a common sense of geography, we are now part of a global tribe. Still trying to adjust to the radical shift in our lives—once a very sedentary people, we have become a highly mobile clan with multiple affiliations—we thrive and prosper. It is that transition, that adding on of identity, that effort to adjust, that I mainly write about, both in fiction and nonfiction.

I think of that tongue-tied refugee child at the blackboard in seventh grade drawing pictures of helicopters and rice paddies, trying to tell his story to his new American classmates, sharing what he remembered, what he had lost. He knew it even before he could fully articulate it: between East and West lay a terrain that needed to be charted by stories, fused by his new eyes and imagination, and he needed to tell those stories if he ever hoped to be whole again. Decades later, I'm happy to report that—dancing at the far end of that continuum—he's still doggedly at it.

ODE TO THE BAY

My first California moment: I am twelve years old. I do not yet speak English, only Vietnamese and French. Fresh from the Pendleton refugee camp, I am, after summer school, quickly enrolled in an ESL class at Colma Junior High, south of San Francisco. On our second day we all learn to parrot this phrase: "I am from…" Thus, shyly, in various accents, the world introduces itself:

…*the Philippines*
…*Mexico*
…*Nicaragua*
….*Greece*
…*Taiwan*
…*Vietnam.*

For my first semester I am wedged between Mexico and Taiwan. Taiwan is timid and bookish, but boisterous Mexico, whose name is Juan, and I immediately bond. Communicating with our hands, facial gestures, and a few shared words, we manage to joke and banter. "I am from Mexico," Juan keeps whispering in various cadences, as if trying out a new song, until I fall into a fit of giggles. Mrs. H., our teacher, who is beautiful and blond, and married to a black man from Africa (she shows us pictures of her wedding the first day), makes us sit outside of the classroom for disrupting the class.

And here's the moment: A redhead stops by as Juan continues his antics outside. "I'm from here," she says, and then she shakes our hands as if we had just landed on the tarmac. "Welcome to America," she says. She then gives us each a stick of cinnamon gum. Juan and I look at each other and shrug. I pop the gum into my mouth and chew.

Spicy. Sweet.

As an American adult I can now finally say what I intuited at that piquant instant: to live in the Bay Area, where I am now from, is to live at the crossroads of a global society. It's many a tourist's mistake to define the place materially, and it is true that the things it is known for—arching bridges and grand ports and famed high-tech companies—evoke, in many ways, what often transpires here: the ability to span distances and transgress borders.

A magnificent terrain, certainly, and full of golden promises, but so much more: a place where human restlessness and fabulous alchemical commingling are becoming increasingly the norm. The entire world comes to the Bay Area, and the Bay Area, in return, assimilates the world. The Central Pacific Railroad ended here, but more than a century and a half later, the majority of the construction of that far-reaching new undertaking, the information highway—Yahoo, Google, IBM, eBay, Cisco Systems, Craigslist, Apple, Pixar, Intel, Oracle, and a myriad of others—while centered here, is everywhere, virtually.

Gertrude Stein once observed about Oakland, where she spent her childhood, that "there's no there there." But having grown up here and traveled the world, I'd like to add this corollary: nowhere is as both here and there as the Bay Area.

Go to the San Francisco International Airport on any given day and you'll see what I mean. A world in motion, in flux: the number of people who pass through those gates at SFO each year exceeds the entire population of the Golden State. At last count, there were 112 languages spoken in the Bay Area, and 80 in the thirty-square-mile city of Richmond, population one hundred thousand. On warm summer afternoons, San Francisco's Nob Hill turns into the modern Tower of Babel. The languages of the world—Chinese, French, Spanish, German, Russian, Thai, Japanese, Hindi, Vietnamese, and many more I do not recognize—waft in through open windows, accompanied by the cable cars' merry cling-clanging bells.

These days Shanghai, Mumbai, Cairo, Paris, Buenos Aires, and the like are much closer to the Bay Area than we ever thought possible. There's a transnational revolution taking place, one right beneath our noses. The teenage girl in Marin County is flirting in the chat room with the teenage boy in Islamabad. The Chinese businessman in Silicon Valley is talking to his grandmother in Guangdong on his cell phone while answering emails to his business partners in London and Rio de Janeiro. And when a woman at a cocktail party told me casually that she was bicoastal, she did not mean the tired New York–San Francisco trajectory. She summers in San Francisco but winters in Shanghai.

Or try on this scene, another California moment: in their high-ceilinged SoMa flat, two friends of mine are conversing with the world. An Austrian H1B Silicon Valley computer whiz chats with his parents in Vienna on his webcam; his Singaporean boyfriend, who is holding his hand, is gossiping in mixed Mandarin and English on his cell phone with his sister in Melbourne. On TV, which neither one is watching at the moment, characters from their favorite Japanese anime are fighting a bloody battle in some futuristic metropolis.

California's diversity is, of course, nothing new. Multiracial, multicultural, and multilingual—even if differences were not historically celebrated, all these delineations were part of the Golden State from the get-go. Native Americans in California were forced to forfeit their lands to early settlers, and another epic collision came when Latin and Anglo America met East Asia, and the result was modern California.

Long before Webster acknowledged the word, globalization had already swept over the Bay Area. Gold made the state famous around the world, and the world rushed in and greeted itself, perhaps for the first time. Since then layers upon layers of complexity—tastes, architecture, religions, animals, plants, stories, music, languages—have been piled onto the place, making it in many ways postmodern even before the rest of the world struggled to enter the modern era.

Before I came to San Francisco I too knew it, as most East Asians knew it, as Old Gold Mountain, with the Golden Gate as entrance to a wondrous America. Living on that mountain now, I too have seen my share of the gold rush made new by microchips and startup companies. "Try to imagine," a Vietnamese American entrepreneur friend of mine tells me, "a new wave of Indians and Chinese and Vietnamese software programmers building the information highway, and you have the repeat of when poor Chinese laborers were building the railroad." Except for this: he retired at thirty-eight, having sold his startup company at the right time, and now manages his portfolio and collects art.

Diversity may not be new, but it has certainly been intensified by the volume of interactions, and by the rate of change we are all experiencing due to the forces of globalization. And new too is the way our society has gone from being overtly xenophobic—many Chinese railroad workers were murdered when they finished building the railroad—to celebratory about our differences. While racism will always lurk in many a resenting heart, and fear of the other will always be part of the human condition, cultures that were once considered proprietary have spilled irrevocably into the mainstream, mixing with one another, transforming the landscape.

In my lifetime here I have watched the pressure to move toward some generic, standardized melting-potted center deflate—transform, in fact—to something quite its opposite, as the demography shifts toward a society in which there's no discernible majority, no clear single center. Being Asian I can't help but notice, of course, the region's undeniable Asian flare. It's therefore not surprising that Kevin, with his Germanic ancestry, is so impressed by the Orient. Or rather, the Orient has for a while now impressed itself upon him. In a Chinese restaurant the other day, he scowled at the French tourist's struggle with her chopsticks over a bowl of shrimp noodle at the next table— a single chopstick in each well-manicured hand, as if she were about to knit. "I have to say, that fucking offends me! It's just so un–San Franciscan."

Which made me laugh. Somehow Kevin's unabashed insistence that chopstick etiquette should be essential to Bay Area living is at once obvious and somehow radical. Which is to also say, if I once felt ashamed of my parents' singsong accents or my mother's strong-scented cooking, or my own Vietnamese memories, I see them now as a norm, as regional colors, if not assets.

Ethnic is chic in a metropolis that grows increasingly horizontal, where ethnic festivals and parades are celebrated publicly with everyone else participating and cheering, and in my mind's eye, they crisscross and stretch into one another, amalgamating toward a hopeful future shimmering at the horizon.

But here, too, is where extreme individualism cohabits with estranged communalism, often within the same block. Tightly knit tribes—Little Saigons, Chinatowns, Little Kabuls—with their own in-language media and temples and churches, exist alongside Latino Muslims, black Buddhists, Mien teenagers speaking Ebonics. Cities meld into one another here, where neighborhoods overlap one another, and where every system— community, company, individual—is opened to various degrees, communicating with every other, and constantly readjusting itself in many marvelous and surprising ways.

This is the age of "hybridity," as coined by G. Pascal Zachary, in which individuals claim multiple memberships. Children born from so much intermixing have coined new words to describe themselves—Blaxicans, Hindjews, Chirish, Afropinos, Caureans, Japoricans, Cambofricans, Chungarians, Zebras, and Rainbows—coinages that confound the standard categories offered by the U.S. Census. What to do indeed when the category of "Other" threatens to be as large as anything like "Black" or "Hispanic" or "Asian"? Lonny Shavelson and Fred Setterberg, authors of the book of photos and essays *Under the Dragon,* remind us that nearly a quarter of UC Berkeley students polled in 2004 identified themselves as "multi-racial or multi-ethnic."

But if the center does not hold, or rather, if we now live in a multi-centered reality, where not just society but individuals themselves have become diverse, with multiple affiliations and memberships, then what possible metaphor can capture it all? Shavelson and Setterberg came up with one: under the flap of the dancing Chinese dragon at the Chinese New Year parade, Latinos and Russian immigrants and Samoans are found dancing along with the Chinese. It is both an apt and poetic image of this new undiscovered country.

But be warned: the horizontal metropolis is not seeking equilibrium. And, like the undulating dragon, it seeks to create new patterns and points of connection in a world that is constantly changing. No one book or essay is therefore enough to capture the enormous complexity of the Bay Area.

After all, here is where, for the first time in human history, all of the world's traditions and ideas are available at close proximity, and with the information of the world compressed and compiled and available at the click of a mouse. Here life can be expansive in its richness as never before, if an individual is open to change.

To live in the Bay Area fully is to learn to see the many dimensions of the world simultaneously; where others hear a cacophony, the resident of cosmopolitan reality discerns a symphony. It entails the ability to overcome the paralysis that may be caused by many conflicting ideas, by finding and inventing new connections between them. It entails fundamental respect for others' histories. Above all, one needs the spirit of adventure and curiosity, and the willingness to hear and embrace others' stories and to recognize in them one's own.

———

One more California moment: Sitting next to me on a jumbo jet coming back from Tokyo, an old woman in her nineties gives in to nostalgia. The orchards she knew as a little girl come flooding back as she peers down at the valley below. She remembers the scent of peach blossoms, a verdant valley, a slow rhythm of life. But oh, how everything changes so quickly. How the peach trees of her youth had transformed into a Valley of Silicon. She is otherwise a kindred soul, an avid traveler. "Have you been away long?" she asks.

"A month," I say. "Not too long, but long enough. I can't wait to come home."

We are almost on the ground. On the speakers, the flight attendant tells us in English, Mandarin, then Japanese to fasten our seatbelts and adjust our seats for the landing. Out the window, beneath our wings, I see the rolling hills of San Francisco, the spanning bridges, the shimmering high-rises, the sparkling bay. But then I feel the gentle touch of my seatmate's wizened hand alighting on my own. "Well," she says, imparting a longstanding local wisdom, "tell you what—it's a new world every time."

WILD, WILD EAST

Picture this sun-drenched memory: I am five years old in white pajamas and swinging on a hammock. The cicadas are humming on the flame trees but I'm not entirely there in the Mekong Delta. In my hands is a thick, worn picture book; I'm on a quest with Monkey King, Pig Monster, and a cranky Water Demon as they search for their kidnapped master in *Journey to the West*—my first martial arts, magic-endowed epic.

That famous, well-loved sixteenth-century yarn came down from far up north—from an equally mythical country called China. Besides Confucianism and Taoism, China gave me clashing swords, flashing silk brocades, and demonic fighters dancing on mountaintops, and for many a childhood siesta I just simply couldn't go to sleep.

Picture, then, another memory: I am nine and being driven to school in an army jeep in Saigon. But today the street is filled with weeping young men donning white headbands. On their shoulders sits a garlanded altar. My jeep draws near. Bruce Lee's handsome photograph stares out of the altar, his face full of confidence and determination. Asia's most famous son died a few days earlier while making a film in Hong Kong. I, too, begin to cry.

Every schoolboy I know loves Bruce Lee, and I am no exception. At school, the older boys often say, "Little Dragon Lee shows the Americans and the French how it is to fight, and what honor really is." Through Little Dragon Lee, we can imagine

ourselves, our own faces, on the silver screen, never mind that
Vietnamese see China as a traditional enemy. Lee transcended
race and national boundaries. In the schoolyard many of us, after
having seen a Bruce Lee movie, would pretend to know martial
arts. We would fight each other under the shade of the tamarind
trees, and repeat certain lines learned from the film, and echo
Bruce Lee's famous high-pitched growl to unnerve our oppo-
nents. Lee single-handedly brought the heroic Asian male image,
long suffering from invisibility, onto the world stage, so how can
I not weep at his passing?

And picture this, my Vietnamese close-up: I am eleven. Communist tanks roll into Saigon. An inveterate bookworm, I read
quickly the last pages of *Demi-Gods and Semi-Devils,* written by
that most famous and prolific of all Wuxia (martial arts) novel-
ists, Jin Yong, whose work inspired several generations of filmmakers and comic book artists across Asia. I toss the book back
through the car's window, grab my backpack, wave good-bye to
Uncle Phuoc, the family chauffeur, and board the C-130 cargo
plane with my mother, sister, and two grandmothers to begin our
lives in exile. On the plane heading toward Guam, amidst weeping refugees, my head remains full of dueling villains and heroes
as my homeland beneath me gives way to a vast green sea. Mythical, magical China accompanies me on my own journey to the
other west: the wild, wild West.

But the America that received my family and me in the mid-
seventies did not yet fathom the dawning of the Pacific Century.
And if Bruce Lee, with his swift kicks and furious punches and
energized grunts, made a dent in the American imagination, he
died too soon and did not save me from the taunts of the neighborhood kids. The blond teenagers who played softball and Fris-
bee mocked my cousins and me. For a few more years yet, we
tried to live out our childhood kung fu fantasies in the backyard
of my parents' new home.

We knew all the lore of martial arts epics: the right acupressure could paralyze one's enemy, the antidote to the deadly flower from the Cave of Desperate Love was the poisonous sting of a certain bee, Wu Tang Clan's secret fighting manual would teach you how to soar high above the treetops and run on the surface of water. "The Iron Palm," "The Eight Holy Dragon Steps," and "The Six-Median Sword Energy"—this was the idiom of our childhood wonders.

Alas, it was not yet a shared language, and it fell on mostly deaf American ears. "How can you paralyze someone with just a finger, that's just so stupid," our young neighbors would jeer over the fence when we tried to explain the great power of various kung fu techniques. Embarrassed, we took our mock kung fu fighting, our heroic quest in ancient China, into the safety of the garage, hidden from neighbors and the glaring Californian sunlight.

Until the Cold War ended, Asian immigrants to America were largely cut off from the narratives of their home continent. News and images from home barely trickled in. A letter from Vietnam took months to arrive. A newspaper from Hong Kong took days to arrive. There was no section of the supermarket that offered spices from Asia.

Out of nostalgia, my cousins and I would sometimes venture to the Great Star Theater, that dingy, moldy barn on the edge of San Francisco Chinatown where kung fu movies were the daily staple. Back then, the stories of revenge and blood debts and the heroes' agonizing endurance, learning martial arts in order to restore their clans' honor and so on, could be seen at a few art houses and, increasingly, through the new invention called the VCR, into which we slipped videotapes from Hong Kong to watch the old Wuxia epics unfold in the comfort of our own homes, dreaming of a lost continent.

But as the century drew to a close, everything changed.

Let's fast-forward a couple of decades or so, toward the new millennium, to an age of unprecedented travel and mass migration and global commerce, where the borders are porous and information, thanks to various high-tech gadgets, flows freely regardless of boundaries and geography, and where the East is now sizzling hot.

Picture this new kung fu moment: Michelle Yeoh and Zhang Ziyi are dueling it out with mind-boggling martial arts skills from one ancient rooftop to another, a steady drumbeat egging them on. Fists and kicks fly, elbows and knees clash, there are back flips and somersaults, and the excited audience at the Sony Metreon Cineplex murmur their collective approval. When that awesome scene is over, they erupt in clamorous cheers. It's Ang Lee's film *Crouching Tiger, Hidden Dragon*, an American production, filmed entirely in Mandarin but shown in thousands of major theatres across the United States—a first. Lee has rendered sophisticated and elegant an old genre, lifting it above its often "chopsocky," low-budget status to the level of poetry.

I must confess, watching the audience's enthusiastic reaction I am of two minds. It is like seeing my own childhood fantasies emerge finally from my parents' dusty garage to spill irrevocably onto the public sphere. I feel terribly proud and excited, but there is also this nagging feeling lurking right underneath, something akin to mourning. In an era when America increasingly relies on the Far East for entertainment and inspiration, my private world, it seems, is private no longer; Asia exudes her mysticism and America is falling slowly under her spell.

Kung fu fighting, once exotic, has become the norm. At the beginning, learning martial arts was the foreground, the underlying plot. Remember David Carradine in the TV series *Kung Fu*, in the early seventies? As Kwai Chang Caine, he learned martial arts in China and then went on to search for his father in America. But these days kung fu fighting is so common that it serves as the background to various movies, television shows, video games, and ads. Turn on the TV and you'll see ads like the one for chatnow.com, where a young woman raises her foot menacingly near a man's head while calmly talking to him, and cartoons like *Kim Possible*, where martial arts fighting seems like the normal routine for teenage girls, as well as children's afternoon shows like *Power Rangers*, cult reruns of *Xena: Warrior Princess* (who can indeed paralyze someone with a touch of her finger!), the ABC hit series *Alias*, and so on. Charlie's new Angels all know martial arts. The new Mr. and Mrs. Smith, Brad Pitt and Angelina Jolie, simply employ their fighting skills to beat each other up as their marriage goes awry. Everybody, to paraphrase Carl Douglas, is kung fu fighting.

So much has changed since Bruce Lee first flew like an avenging god across the silver screen in his awe-inspiring kick. Lee not only introduced martial arts to the West, he redefined cinematic language itself. Gone is the old idea that bigger is better. Swiftness and a precise kick can topple mass. Agility proves superior to brawn. The body in martial arts motion is pure art, an acrobatic dance endowed with a kind of lethal elegance and grace that had not, up until Bruce Lee, been imagined for cinematic fights.

The Hong Kong movie industry in the late eighties and early nineties took Bruce Lee's legacy a few steps further. While it lagged behind Hollywood for a long time, the Hollywood of the East, as it was known, suddenly made movies that "not only astonished people, but more important, [were] unrestrained, free ranging and unburdened by tradition," according to Li Cheuk-to, writing for *Cinemaya*. Jackie Chan did amazing stunts and became a globe-trotting cop, and Michelle Yeoh could kick backward over her shoulder to dispose of an opponent, while everyone else too tried to outdo each other with their kung fu skills on-screen and with their imaginative cinematography, one movie more inventive and fantastic than the next.

During this golden era, which began to fade after China took over in 1997, Hong Kong movies reminded David Overbey, writing in *Film Comment* magazine, of Hollywood in its heyday, "before the great split between commerce and art." The decisive breakthrough in action movies came in the early 1990s with productions like *Once Upon a Time in China* and *Swordsman II* and *A Chinese Ghost Story*, in which characters are playful and barely affected by gravity. Dueling fighters float like birds in the air, wearing fantastical costumes and following a story line even more fanciful than their clothing: a cult leader absorbs chi power from lesser fighters and shrinks them to nothing; energy bolts come through swords to split a horse in two; a fighter achieves superpower but in the process must castrate himself and, in Hong Kong's new gender-bending motif, turn into a beautiful woman.

Anything can happen in these movies, and the eye-blurring fighting reaches a level that can only be called superb, surreal, and balletic. The new narrative seems to reflect a sense of uninhibited wildness, and many characters—powerful eccentrics—live outside the social norms and stifling traditions, taking only what's good and discarding the rest. The movies were beginning to examine and explore and deconstruct Confucian ideas, and along with it, issues of loyalty and patriotism and friendship and love. Hong Kong, after all, like the rest of the globalized world, was moving into the age of options; its kung fu movies crossed multiple genres, and the story lines, along with the poetic choreography, were often so stunning and clever that they left an indelible mark on the rest of the world.

Sadly, that period of renaissance ended all too soon. The last time I visited Hong Kong, the theater near my hotel was playing solely American films, from *The Blair Witch Project* to *The General's Daughter* to *The Sixth Sense*. If I had expected sword-toting heroes flying on rooftops, gangster girls using guns and knives to take over each other's casinos, or beautiful ghosts in fabulous kimonos falling in love with handsome but hapless travelers, I was out of luck. It didn't help that rampant video piracy had cut the dwindling profit margin to near nothing while Bangkok and Seoul and even Mainland China had begun to turn into bona fide new centers for filmmaking, including fabulous martial arts movies. Seoul, in time, became the new Hollywood of the Far East, its glamorous stars and pop singers commanding mass continental appeal, its soap operas translated into a dozen Asian languages.

Hong Kong's loss, however, was Hollywood's gain. John Woo, considered by many to be the best of the Hong Kong cop-and-robber filmmakers, was the first to move to Hollywood in the mid-nineties, and he stayed. Woo turned the likes of Tom Cruise and Jean-Claude Van Damme and Nicolas Cage into slick action heroes. Soon Woo was followed by many of his compatriots. The mega-hit *The Matrix* also benefited from the Far East. Not only did it borrow ideas from the Japanese anime series *Ghost in the Shell,* it also gained greatly from a team of Hong Kong martial arts choreographers. Chief among them was Yuen Wo-ping, a martial arts master who also shaped the careers of Jet Li and Jackie Chan. It's as if all the cinematic and martial arts skills that Hong Kong filmmakers had incorporated in the previous three decades were applied to render Keanu Reeves, the hapa star—part Asian, part white—who played a Neo-Christ/ Buddha in a futuristic world ruled by machines, as a stunningly skilled martial artist.

If Hong Kong was once known for borrowing indiscriminately from Hollywood movies, the reverse has now happened. Its martial arts genre has inspired the West, where it continues to evolve. Oliver Stone, Francis Ford Coppola, Quentin Tarantino, and many other directors have all expressed tremendous enthusiasm for the martial arts genre. Tarantino, who watched Hong Kong movies while working in a video store before finding fame, drew heavily on John Woo's film *City on Fire* in making his first film,

Reservoir Dogs. A longtime fan of Hong Kong movies, he revolutionized Hollywood with his relentless pace, his bloody but often humorous movies. *Kill Bill* 1 and 2, for instance, are his tribute to Shaw Brothers kung fu movies, to the TV series *Kung Fu,* and to his own movies, from *Pulp Fiction* to *Reservoir Dogs.* In the first *Kill Bill,* Uma Thurman plays a swordswoman rising from a coma to take revenge on an assassin posse to which she once belonged. She wears a yellow jumpsuit just like the one Bruce Lee wore more than three decades before in *Fist of Fury,* she searches for a good sword, she improves her martial arts skills, and she hacks dozens of men to death in scene after scene. The audience laughs when bodies are chopped and blood spurts. No one can oppose Thurman in her wrath.

Tarantino leads the pack in reinventing the old genre, turning the slash-and-smash form into something that is all at once replete with not only a traditional plot, but also homage and satire. The old kung fu movie has gone through radical changes over the years, entering the age of postmodernism, and has matured to the point where it draws a huge following even when it is poking fun at itself.

So here's the thing: West has become part of East. Yoga is the new aerobics (my instructor is a redhead) and acupuncture is now accepted by HMOs (my favorite acupuncturist is French). Many women and men of American letters now have South Asian or Chinese last names, which is no longer new. You can find fish sauce and wasabi down the aisle in Safeway. Turn on the TV and the Food Network will teach you how to make pho soup and Thai curry. Asian cultures have become so much part of America that they're tattooed as Chinese or Sanskrit characters on alabaster skin, and often it's non-Asian Americans who peddle Asian cultures to everyone, including Asians.

Kung Fu Panda, a Steven Spielberg production, was a blockbuster smash in China. The animated film was so popular that many Chinese thinkers and writers wondered why China couldn't make the same movie. As one Chinese critic observed, "The panda and kung fu are China's treasures, but we have to let foreigners remind us of that." And please, don't get him and his colleagues started on Disney's *Mulan!*

Another case in point: the animated television series *Avatar: The Last Airbender*, wherein a boy wakes up a hundred years into the future and finds his whole race gone, and he must bring balance back to the world, is also produced by Americans, Michael Dante DiMartino and Bryan Konietzko. They both admit to borrowing wildly from Asian themes: from martial arts to Taoist ideas of elemental manipulation to Hindu ideas of reincarnation to the mature themes of revenge, death, genocide, and love with which Japanese manga and anime are often infused.

It is astounding to think of a new generation of American children growing up not with innocuous Bugs Bunny or Tom and Jerry but with an array of adult narratives from Japan: complex and often terrifying themes of war and destruction and revenge along with their new cartoon characters, many of whom are well versed in martial arts. But such are the marvels of the renewed New World, in which we all continually renegotiate the meaning of pluralism.

After all, one does not believe in the effects of feng shui and acupuncture without eventually recognizing the chi, that mysterious force ancient Taoist priests saw flowing through the universe. One does not practice yoga and meditation without making some kind of inroad into the nature of the enlightened mind, the way ancient yogis saw it. One does not practice martial arts seriously without embodying the mindset of ancient martial arts warriors: years of practice and endurance, and the will of steel.

East and West—the twain have met with the blessing of shared fascination. A refugee to California, I once resigned myself to the idea that incense smoke, gongs, and Confucian dramas were simply an Asian immigrant's preoccupation, a private affair of sorts. But I've changed my mind.

Picture this, my new kung fu moment: I am at my writing desk, typing in the early morning, my oolong tea beside me. But I'm not fully there. I'm in a land where cultures intersect and traditions crisscross, between swords flashing on ancient, lichen-covered temple rooftops and cars zooming down double-tiered freeways. Like the heroes of old, I carry on my skills, walking a path with determination to tell my stories. Language is my weapon, invention my martial art. I seek to marry the New World to the Old Continent, fantasies to memories, and, through the act of writing, reimagine the hemispheres as one.

MY TEACHER, MY FRIEND

The year I reached puberty was also the year I became an American teenager, and the man who stood at the entrance to my New World was my first English teacher. Ernie Kaeselau was his name. He passed away recently, and though I hadn't seen him in more than three decades, the news of his demise left me unexpectedly bereft.

I remember a warm voice, expressive eyes, and bushy eyebrows that wiggled comically at a pun or a joke. I remember someone who treated me with care, made me feel special when I—a stranger on a new shore—was terribly lost and bewildered.

Having fled Saigon in spring of 1975 during finals in sixth grade, I landed in San Francisco a couple months later and attended summer school at Colma Junior High in Daly City, preparing myself for seventh grade. Never mind that I didn't speak English, only Vietnamese and passable French, and that two days after my mother, grandmothers, sister, and I left in a cargo plane, communist tanks came crashing through the gates of the Independence Palace in Saigon, and the war ignominiously ended. Never mind that in those few months before arriving in San Francisco I subsisted in two refugee camps and spent most of my nights in a tent praying for the safety of my father and other relatives and friends who remained behind.

I never knew what Mr. K's politics were—liberal is my guess—and if I had any then, ours would have surely clashed when it came to the politics of Vietnam. But when it came to me—the first Vietnamese refugee in his classroom—his policy was plenary kindness.

Mr. K's first question was my name and his second was how to properly pronounce it in Vietnamese. He asked me to repeat this several times until, to my surprise, he got the complicated intonation almost right. A day or two later, he asked again and practiced it until it was perfect, and soon thereafter, the Vietnamese refugee boy became the American teacher's pet. It was my task to go get his lunch, erase the blackboard, and collect and distribute homework assignments. When I missed the bus, which was often, and sometimes deliberately, he'd drive me home, a privilege that was the envy of the other kids.

Back in my homeland, I used to bow when meeting a teacher. As a grade school student, with arms folded in front and eyes staring at my sandaled feet, I would mumble, *"Thua thay!"*— Greetings, Teacher! In fact, it took me half a year or so after having arrived in America to stop that kowtowing habit, which my American classmates in seventh grade found either funny or quite bizarre.

And I found them strange as well. American kids wore colorful clothes, smoked in the bathroom, and swore at each other and, sometimes, even at their teachers—something unheard of in Vietnamese tradition. At first I was terrified, fearful of the big, rowdy kids of all races who got into bloody fights in the schoolyard. But Mr. K's classroom was a haven. Lunchtime and the "good kids" made a beeline for it. Away from the schoolyard bullies, we ate our lunch, played games, and did our homework. I remember plenty of laughter, arguments, gossip, and, yes, even budding flirtations, and Mr. K reigned over the chaos with ease, sitting behind his desk, reading a newspaper or helping one of us with our assignments.

For a while, I was his echo. "Sailboat," he would say while holding a card up in front of me with an image of a sailboat on it, and "sailboat," I would repeat after him, copying his inflection and facial gestures. "Hospital," he would say, with another card held up. And "hospital," I would yell back like a little parrot. I listened to his diction. I listened to the way he enunciated certain words when he read passages from a book. If he could say my Vietnamese name, surely I could bend my tongue to make myself sound more American.

That first summer, he gave me A's that didn't count. He took our little group bowling, formed a little team, taught us how to keep score, and bought us soft drinks. Then, he took us on a field trip to a baseball game, my first. He took his time to explain to me the intricacies of the game. It was followed by a trip to Sonoma to see wineries and cheese factories. I remember crossing the Golden Gate Bridge for the first time, with Mr. K's voice narrating its history, how it was built, and I remember that I asked him afterward, in broken English, if it was made of real gold, and the entire bus erupted in laughter.

Most memorable, however, were the books that came in a carton. Along with the bowling team, Mr. K had formed a little book club. And for a few dollars, we—children of the working class and immigrants—became owners of a handful of books. The box came one morning in the middle of class, and it felt a bit like Christmas in July. We jostled each other to be up front at his desk as Mr. K read the title of each book out loud, then matched the book with the name of its owner. My first book was *The Wind in the Willows*, by Kenneth Grahame, and I remember poring over its pristine pages in wonder. Wasn't it then that the smell of fresh ink, paper, and glue became indelibly for me the smell of yearning and imagination? I did not yet know how to read in English—but oh, how impatient I was to learn!

That summer, I bought my first typewriter from a cantankerous junkman whose inventory was down the street and who my family was fond of calling "Old Angry Junkman." It cost $1.25

and some keys didn't work very well and the ribbon had long ago faded. Nevertheless, I typed out Kenneth Grahame's famous tale about Mole, who left his underground home and went up for air and ended up sailing down the river toward adventures. I read many sentences from *The Wind in the Willows* out loud as I typed. Precocious, perhaps, but by the time I joined seventh grade in the fall, I was something of a typist and a reader of the English-language novel.

If I pushed myself so hard to move forward, I had plenty of good reasons: In Vietnam, I was a child of an upper-class family, insulated in a world of villas, lycée, servants, walled gardens, and sports clubs. In America, I was the son of impoverished refugees who subsisted with another refugee family in a ramshackle apartment near the end of Mission Street, where the promises of San Francisco ended and the working-class world of Daly City began. My homeland abruptly evaporated, and my family and clan were torn apart, and my sheltered life was gone. Thrust upon an alien world, I understood intuitively that I had best run far and fast if I were to leave all my losses behind.

Thus, my world split into two: at night I wept myself to sleep, longing for my lost world, for my father, dreaming a recurring dream of a Saigon in smoke and myself abandoned in an old villa as the Viet Cong ransacked the city; but in the daytime—in school, at lunch, in English and art classes—I became a rowdy, giggly boy, chatting up a storm. I remember talking, a lot. When my vocabulary failed me, I resorted to using French words or drawing in my notebook or on the blackboard to convey my ideas and thoughts.

Within a few months, I began to speak English freely, though haltingly, and outgrew Mr. K's cards. I began to banter and joke with my new friends. I acquired a new personality, a sunny, sharp-tongued kid, and often Mr. Kaeselau would shake his head and marvel at the transformation. I remember his astonished face when I argued against the class clown and won; my tongue was being sharpened even if my sentences remained fragmented.

I made friends—Samoans, whites, blacks, Filipinos, Chinese, Mexicans. I wrote valentine cards to giggly girls. I joined the school newspaper, became something of a cartoonist. My second year in America, I was getting straight A's, no fake A's needed anymore, thank you. I joined the honors club. I found my bearings; because it affectionately absorbed me, I enthusiastically embraced it. I was becoming, as my mother complained to my father, who had escaped Vietnam on a naval ship and joined us, "an American brat."

———

Here's what some classmates wrote in my eighth grade yearbook, one that I, since I was on the yearbook staff, helped design.

"Have fun talking your mouth off at Jefferson [high school] and maybe next year I'll go to the 'Lam' dunk contest…"

"To someone who is always talking. Have a nice time at Jefferson…"

"To a kid who was so loud in art [class] and wore funny hats…"

"Hope you never change from the kid I knew from Colma. The little but cool Vietnamese I used to go to school with…"

On its last page, in the lower lefthand corner, Mr. K, in his succinct and modest way, left this note:

"To my good Friend. It's been a pleasure to be your teacher & friend for 2 years. Don't forget to keep me informed of your progress. Ernie Kaeselau."

When I graduated from junior high, I went to say good-bye to Mr. Kaeselau and he gave me the old cue cards to take home as mementos, knowing full well that I didn't need them anymore. That day, a short day, I remember taking a shortcut over a hill. On the way down, I tripped and fell. The cards flew out of my hand to scatter like a flock of playful butterflies on the verdant slope. Though I skinned my knee, I laughed. Then, as I scampered to retrieve the cards, I found myself yelling out ecstatically the name of each image on each one of them— "school," "cloud," "bridge," "house," "dog," "car"—as if for the first time.

It was then that I looked up and saw, far in the distance, San Francisco's downtown, its glittering high-rises resembling a fairy-tale castle made of diamonds, with the shimmering sea dotted with sailboats as backdrop.

"City," I said, "my beautiful city." And the words rang true; they slipped into my bloodstream and I was suddenly overwhelmed by an intense hunger. I wanted to swallow the breathtaking landscape before me.

But that was that, as they say. And I sailed on.

For it turned out I didn't go to Jefferson, where many of my closest friends ended up. I went to Serramonte High, an awful, unchallenging school known for its smoking pit and frequent robberies in bathrooms. But thanks to a relative whose address was in a coveted zip code, I transferred to Lowell High School—a prestigious public school in San Francisco. Superior to any school around, Lowell provided high achievement standards and advanced-placement courses. I made new friends and ended up at UC Berkeley. That is to say, I left the working-class world where Mission Street ended and worked myself toward where Mission Street began, toward the city's golden promises—and it is in one of those glittering glassy towers by the water that I live now.

I didn't bother to look back, didn't bother to keep my mentor and friend abreast of my progress. Several decades later, a seasoned journalist and essayist who had traveled the world a few times, I, on one whimsical weekend, decided to write an article about learning English, and Mr. K was featured prominently.

Did I know that Mr. K read and treasured that article? Did I know that he, in retirement, kept coming back to it, to my writing—to me?

No. Not until his best friend, another teacher, sent me this note to inform me of his passing:

Most of us know what pleasure Ernie got from your article. While he was proud he was also a modest man.....He sent copies to many relatives back East. I'm sure he couched it in pride for what you have accomplished, but he was deeply honored. What no one knows is he was a bit unhappy that there was no retirement recognition. He told me many times he didn't want any big deal, but as the years passed, he would speak somewhat wistfully of the lack of acknowledgement. You gave him acknowledgement.

To be honest, it never occurred to me to see the story from Mr. K's angle. When I tried to see the classroom from behind his desk as the years streamed by—student after student, generation after generation—I could not see myself standing out. I might have been the first Vietnamese refugee to turn up in his classroom, but I was not the last. My cousins came, so did others, and surely, later on, other needy, traumatized refugee children from other bloody conflicts. I might have been precocious, but how could I have possibly stood out to a man who taught for decade after decade?

I had grieved for my lost homeland, for many other things. I had traveled to distant lands, to war zones, and even back to Vietnam to say my proper good-byes to my interrupted childhood, but I didn't go back to where Mission Street ended, to where that little junior high stood at the foot of the mountains amid cemeteries often veiled in the morning fog. Living nearby, I had felt, unreasonably, that were I to drive down Mission Street and peek through the window of my mentor's classroom, he would still be there—that Mr. K would *always* be there, making other needy kids feel special, and that there would always be little bowling teams and little book clubs in the summer and rowdy speed tournaments at lunchtime. And in dreams and reveries, haven't I revisited him countless times?

But that's the trouble with childhood, isn't it, especially happy ones? Happy children don't question their contentment any more than fish wonder about the river's current; they swim on. My childhood, interrupted by war, was rekindled by kindness, and instead of cynicism and bitterness, my curiosity and imagination took hold and kept growing in the New World. And because I felt blessed and happy, I went on blessedly with my business of growing up. Mr. K opened America's gate and ushered me in, and I, so hungry for all its possibilities, rushed through it.

"I think your leading off would be very appropriate unless it makes you uncomfortable," wrote Mr. K's friend. "Lord knows I heard him talk about you several times. He kept mentioning it near the end."

———

The retired teachers sat on their pews to somber organ music. Wizened, gray-haired, they rose, one by one, moving slowly, some in arthritic pain, to speak with affection and humor of a man who was known as much for his aesthetic sensibilities and practical jokes and friendship as he was for his devotion to the art of teaching and to his students. Shared memories echoed inside the gilded columbarium like some ode to beauty itself...

He was a talented organist...loved driving cross-country...Spanish architecture and colonial history of California...this thing where he mimicked people while walking behind them...created beautiful stained glass objects...collected antique silver and botanical prints...

He was especially fond of orchids...

To all this I would say still that his greatest talent was empathy: he intuited how one felt and, like a bodhisattva, performed his magic to assuage grief.

But if there's a sad statement about the American scholastic experience it is that the passing of a beloved teacher is often not mourned by his or her students, but by, if he or she were any good, mostly peers. Father's Day and Mother's Day are remembered, but a good teacher, alas, rarely receives a card from his former students on Teacher's Day. Drinking coffee and eating finger sandwiches after the service, I kept asking anyone younger than me if he or she had been a student of Mr. K. And the answer was always no.

"Teaching is not a lost art," the historian Jacques Barzun once observed, "but the regard for it is a lost tradition." The refugee boy not only led, as it turned out: he was the only former student of Ernie Kaeselau's to cry at his memorial.

———

Suddenly he stood by the edge of a full-fed river....All was a-shake and a-shiver—glints and gleams and sparkles, rustle and swirl, chatter and bubble. The Mole was bewitched, entranced, fascinated. By the side of the river he trotted as one trots, when very small, by the side of a man who holds one spellbound by exciting stories.

I did not fully appreciate the beauty of Grahame's words. Yet even then, not sure of what I read and typed, I knew that it had something to do with me—who, like Mole, albeit against my will, had also left my insulated world and sailed toward the unknown. I also knew by the end of that first summer that I too, for having set out unflinching, would be rewarded with friendship and new ways of seeing things.

A charmed life is one that goes down a river not knowing what's beyond the bend, but confident nevertheless that gracious strangers will be there in one form or another to aid and abet and be a guide through turbulent waters. Charmed was how I felt when I first came here and more than three decades later, charmed is how I feel today—and much of that, I will acknowledge, has to do with Mr. K.

And so—the river glints and sparkles and I sail on. Because I did not go back, I will send ahead to the further stretch where I cannot yet go, to where the storyteller's flesh crumbles to dust but his stories, when told from the heart, may yet live on. For this, tendered by enchanted memories and tinged with regrets, is a story of requited love.

WATERLOO

There's a moment from many years ago that remains indelible on my mind. I don't remember much on our way there to Waterloo, except that the countryside was streaked and blurred, light green over darker green, all under a persistent gray sky.

Father drove. My older sister sat next to him and navigated, a map on her lap. A pouting teenager, I sat behind with Mother, who complained of a mild headache and wondered out loud why we needed to find this distant battlefield, and why we couldn't go freshen up at our hotel after having just arrived in Belgium.

"It would be dark by the time we got to Waterloo had we gone to the hotel!" Father snapped. I didn't have to turn to know Mother was rolling her eyes. If she had a choice she would have been at the hotel and would not have been stuck in the backseat as we searched for some pasture where long ago Napoleon was defeated.

I thought I saw a sign in French. I said so to Father. Except it took me five minutes to get around to doing this. He cursed, calling me names in French. I responded in French, rather rudely, which surprised him since I rarely spoke the language after we came to America.

I felt terrible afterwards, and the air in the car was tense. I remember thinking, were we still in the war and I his subordinate, Father, as a three-star general in the South Vietnamese army, no doubt would have me confined to the brig for whatever it was that I said. But it was half a dozen years since the Vietnam War ended and we'd already turned into an American family on a European vacation, complete with a sulky teenager stuck in the backseat and his responsible but equally sullen sister stuck in front, while their quarreling parents kept at it.

We finally stopped and asked for directions. Father drove frantically after that. We arrived at Waterloo at last—and it was still bright out when he, my sister, and I rushed up the windswept knoll that overlooked the battlefield. Mother declined the climb and went to the shop to buy souvenirs instead.

As we climbed, Father could barely hide his excitement. When we finally stood on top, almost out of breath, he began to narrate the story of the old battle. He pointed wildly: where Napoleon's army stood, which direction the Prussian soldiers came from, and how the Duke of Wellington arrived with his Anglo-Allied forces to turn the tide, defeating Father's favorite military tactician and ultimately exiling him to St. Helena, where he died a few years later.

"It rained before the battle," he was saying. "It delayed Napoleon, you see, he wanted the ground would dry out a little before the attack." Wellington's army was positioned on Mt. St Jean but they withstood repeated attacks. By nightfall they counterattacked and drove the French from the field. Then the Prussians broke through Napoleon's right flank as his army was pulling back. There were heavy losses on all sides.

I already knew the story. I also knew that Father was, in part, trying to make up for cursing at me by telling the old story. It occurred to me that my older brother would have enjoyed this trip far more than me, had he come, and it also occurred to me later that never once had Father told any of his children a fairy tale, and that most likely he remembered none. But this story of a long-ago battle he had told many times, turning our dining room table into the battlefield, our spoons and chopsticks into battalions, bowls into hills. The Duke of Wellington was drunk.

Napoleon was not. But there was nothing he could do, was there, against fate?

My father was second in command at I Corps near the end of the war. He was fighting at the DMZ and nearly lost his life but managed to escape back to Saigon. He boarded a naval ship on the day Saigon fell and headed for Guam. After four years in America, in a remarkable feat, he had remade himself at age forty-six into a bank executive. Yet Father's passion remains extraterritorial. Life in America turned out to be, for him and for my mother, a big letdown, a reality defined by disappointment and a deep sense of loss. They would never have in America what had been taken from them in Vietnam.

For years their biography of sorts was on display on the mantel in the living room: framed black-and-white photos that my brother managed to take with him, as a foreign student in the U.S., before the war ended. In one photo, Father is emerging from his helicopter, silver baton in his left hand, his right reaching out to a young army officer who stands with hunched shoulders under the whirling rotor blades that send wind to press down on the elephant grass. In the distance are the silhouettes of bent-backed farmers in conical hats. Father's face is dark and somber.

In another: Mother and Father. "A beautiful couple" would be understating it. She wears her multistranded gold bead necklace outside her lavender brocade. She looks stunning and regal. Father, on the thin side, is dignified and suave in a gray silk suit, a cigarette in his hand. The picture is most definitely posed. It is the first day of Tet. Behind them, two Chinese brush paintings hang on the wall, one showing a gathering of Chinese fairies on clouds, the other a ferocious dragon descending from a misty mountain.

I don't know why, but sometimes when I think of that picture I have a flashback to being a little boy, hiding inside Mother's walk-in closet, the size of a small room, with windows opened and the breeze swaying the hundred or so painted and embroidered *ao dai* dresses and brocades. I can still smell the camphor and Mother's perfume, Guerlain. I am lost amid the fabric. From far away I hear my brother's voice calling out: "Father's home! Father's home!"

None of the pictures show how it all ended. There are plenty of those online, under "Fall of Saigon" or "April 30, 1975," "Vietnam evacuation," "Evacuation+Saigon." Tens of thousands of them. Tanks rolling into Saigon; helicopters flying out to awaiting American ships; fear-stricken Vietnamese climbing over the barbed wire walls of the U.S. embassy. There are many pictures of refugees in crowded cargo planes landing in the Philippines, and I suppose somewhere there are pictures of me and my mother and sister and two grandmothers emerging from one of those planes with small bags in our hands, looking very, very lost.

I remember much of the day we left: the wails of a woman, the smell of vomit, night turning into day then back into night, the humming of the plane's engines, then we landed in Subic Bay. Then there's another flight to Guam. Then green tents flapping in the wind, a scorching sun, a very long line for food, adults weeping and screaming as the BBC announces the fall of Saigon.

Father left after us, on a warship with hundreds of well-placed others, for the U.S. Navy base at Subic Bay and asylum. He folded away his army uniform, changed into a pair of jeans and a T-shirt, and tossed his gun into the sea.

After that, Vietnam, his defeat, his raison d'être, his crucible, was never far from his consciousness. The war, his role in it, have become for him the touchstone of his life. He knows wars, studies wars, has read countless books on battle strategies and warfare. And Napoleon is his hero.

After so many years of hearing about Napoleon, it should have been exciting seeing the place finally, yet that late summer afternoon I was no longer intrigued. I was homesick for California.

I missed my lover terribly, my first love—our tender kisses, the smell of our sweat. I kept replaying our visit to the ocean, with the breeze carrying the smell of the ocean, how shy we both were, yet how inextricably drawn we were to one another, the orange-red sunset and an unfinished sand castle between us. All I could think of, the entire trip, was getting back to California to possess, to love.

This was why it had taken me a long time to process that we were going in the wrong direction. It was also why, while Father talked on, I was miles away. It was only when he himself stopped talking and looked out to the far-off distance, to where I supposed Napoleon fled, that I turned to look too.

But I didn't see anything resembling a battlefield. What I saw was a thin gray mist drifting lazily over a green pasture below, and in the cold air I smelled a musky odor of newly upturned earth. The pastoral scene at twilight stirred in me no martial passion, but instead poetry, and an unspeakable yearning.

Father talked on. His hair was tousled by the wind, his face contemplative. As I watched him, the image came to me suddenly of him on that naval ship near the Philippines. The government of the Philippines wouldn't let the South Vietnamese ship dock unless all personnel turned in their arms. I imagined him, his face creased with contemplation as he stared at his gun for some time before tossing it into the churning sea below.

Something, a welling, a sharp pain, rose suddenly within me then, and it surprised me that I hadn't felt anything like it before, and it felt close to pity. It lodged in my throat and it took some effort not to cry out loud. There on the wind-blown hill, with the statue of a lion on a pedestal above us as a memorial for all fallen soldiers, Father seemed so utterly alone. But then suddenly, so was I. Frightened and full of my own inarticulate longings, I had to look away for fear that Father might see tears brim in my eyes and think that I, too, was mourning for Napoleon's defeat.

Was it not then that my life turned? Was it not then that I, still owned by a collective sense of loss, nevertheless took some profound step out from under his shadow?

I went on to college in the fall, in any case, and then, after bouts of bickering with my parents, on to my own writing life, following my own passion. I've been to Europe a few times since then, to Amsterdam and even to Brussels, and though I'd think about it, even entertain the idea, not once did I feel compelled to visit that old battlefield again.

ONE ASIAN WRITER'S LESSON: LOVE YOUR IMMIGRANT PARENTS, FOLLOW YOUR BLISS

One summer afternoon many years ago I came home to rob my parents of their American dream. I had graduated from Berkeley with a degree in biochemistry and spent two years in a cancer research lab while preparing myself for med school. But despite friends' coaxing and my parents' ardent expectations, my heart wasn't in it. More important, it had found refuge in literature.

Unbeknownst to them, I had taken several UC extension courses in creative writing and was, to my own surprise, excelling. After reading one of my short stories, Helen, my first creative writing teacher, decided that I was to be a writer. "Andrew, you are *not* going to medical school," she declared in her regal voice, with its clear and precise diction. "You are going to creative writing school!" To which I stammered, "But—but my mom is going to kill me!" Yet I applied anyway and was accepted in the graduate program in creative writing at San Francisco State University.

When I broke the news to my parents the air went out of the living room, and a pall settled in. Mother covered her mouth and cried; Father muttered a few curses in French. My older brother, a civil engineer, shook his head in disgust and left the room. I sat silent but defiant, though inside I was trembling. Here was a nearly irresolvable conflict: I had decided to follow my passion instead of obeying my family's dictum. Though we'd adapted and changed in America, the concept of filial piety, the idea that the collective assigns and directs the destiny of the individual, was still the overarching impetus that operated within our fold.

Pragmatism, besides, defined all of us newcomers who still struggled toward America's middle class. At Berkeley more than half of the Vietnamese Student Association, to which I belonged, majored in computer science and electrical engineering. A few told me they didn't want to become engineers. These fields were highly competitive and difficult. Some wanted to become artists or architects, and a couple of them had ample talents to do so, but their parents were steadfast against it—or worse yet, their families were living still in impoverished Vietnam and were in dire need of their financial support. One in particular was an "anchor kid," someone whose family had sold practically everything they owned to buy him a passage on an escaping boat. Now, alone in the U.S., he had the burden of having to support his family back home while going to school full-time. If he didn't succeed, well, it could very well mean life and death for his starving family back home.

In Vietnam, indeed, an army of hungry, ambitious, and capable young men and women were dying to take his place, and for him, who had barely survived his perilous journey across the South China Sea, "dying to" was no mere idiomatic expression.

Many of my friends were driven by an iron will to achieve academic success. While our dorm-mates put up posters of movie stars and sports heroes, another Vietnamese friend put up his own drawing of a Mandarin in silk brocade and hat. Flanked by soldiers carrying banners, the young mandarin sat on an ornate carriage while peasants stood on the side and cheered. It was a visual sutra that would help my friend focus on his studies.

We had just met then, and when he saw me looking at his painting he said, "*Do trang nguyen ve lang*"—Vietnamese for "Mandarin returns home after passing the Imperial exam." But he didn't need to explain. Like many Asian students from Confucian-bound countries—Vietnam, Taiwan, Singapore, Korea, Japan, and of course, China—I could easily decipher the image. In some ways, for us scholarship boys, it is the equivalent of Michael Jordan flying in the air like a god doing a slam-dunk—a dream of glorious academic achievements.

Then there was me. My parents found jobs when I was barely in my teens and by the time I was about to graduate from high school, they had moved us to a five-bedroom home with a pool at the northern edge of Silicon Valley. Through extraordinary discipline, Father had gotten an MBA while working full-time at the Bank of America and was moving steadily up its ladder. My older brother was working for the city of San Jose and my sister was getting into accounting work just like my mother. I, the youngest, didn't have to make money to send home to some impoverished relatives in Vietnam. In fact, my family had to support me when I went to Berkeley. There were no financial demands on me, no material burdens.

But there were such things as familial honor and debt; and no matter how removed I was from my roots, part of me felt like I was betraying all my family's hard work and expectations by veering toward an unknown path that could very well lead to dismal failure and collective shame.

Filial piety is an ethos that was ingrained long before I set foot on the American shore. It is in essence the opposite of individualism. "Father's benefaction is like Mount Everest, Mother's love like the water from the purest source" is the first adage we Vietnamese children sang in first grade. If American teenagers long to leave home, to turn eighteen to be free and to find themselves, Vietnamese children are taught to fulfill and honor their filial obligations, and on top of that list is education.

As Mother wept, Father issued a challenge: "I wanted to write too, you know, when I was young. I studied French poetry and philosophy. But do you think I could feed our family on poems? Can you name a Vietnamese who's making a living as an American writer? What makes you think *you* can do it?"

I wasn't prepared for his slew of questions. I wracked my brain, trying to come up with one name—and couldn't. This was the late eighties, barely fifteen years into our expulsion from Vietnam, and the vast majority in our community were first-generation immigrants. Many were boat people who had come long after the war ended and had subsisted for years in various camps in Southeast Asia. They were still trying to learn English and make ends meet, and to overcome the horrors they had experienced—no one, as far I as knew, was making a living writing in English.

"I can't name one," I answered. "There may be none right now. So, I'll be the first."

If I felt trapped in a modern Confucian drama, my answer nevertheless came off as defiant and cocksure. Father looked at me—I mean *looked*. It was not an answer he'd expected: it was not how I talked in the family, which is to say, respectful and vaguely compliant for the most part. Perhaps for the first time, he was assessing me anew.

Something was changing inside me: I matched his gaze. At once thrilled and terrified, I had just taken a major step toward some mystery that was going to be The Rest of My Life. I had articulated myself past a significant threshold. If I didn't put all my effort into making it as a writer, I knew then, my own integrity and character would be at stake. Going back to studying for the MCAT and the wretched albino mice, to the petri dishes and the constant buzz of the ventilator in the sterile cancer research lab where hunchbacked scientists in stained lab coats toiled away under desultory fluorescent lights—all that was no longer an option unless I accepted defeat.

———

But why is education so deeply ingrained in the Confucian culture?

Long before America existed, something of the American dream already had taken root in East Asia through the scholarship and examination system of Imperial China, which determined who among the population would be permitted to enter the state's bureaucracy. Villages and towns pooled resources and sent their best and brightest to compete at the Imperial court, hoping that one of their own would make it to the center of power.

Mandarins of various ranks were selected by how well they fared on extremely rigorous examinations that occurred every four years. The brilliant few who passed ran the day-to-day operations of Imperial China. Vietnam, since it was ruled by China and considered to be one of its tributary states, fell under the same system. A mandarin could become a governor or a judge, or he could even marry into the royal family, depending on his prospects. A brilliant peasant with indomitable determination could rise far above his station, elevating the status of his entire clan in the process and bringing honors to the spirits of his ancestors. And it all hinged on his ability to pass the difficult exams. The Imperial exam was an egalitarian vision with national appeal, and education became a universal passion.

Of all the temples in Hanoi, Vietnam's capital, the most beautiful is Van Mieu, the Temple of Literature, dedicated to all those laureates who passed the extremely rigorous Imperial exams of centuries past and became mandarins, their names etched on stone steles that went back nearly eight hundred years. It was Vietnam's first university, known as the Imperial Academy, and eventually it became a temple, a befitting trajectory in a region where education is literally worshipped.

Under French colonial rule not much changed, except females were allowed to move up the scholastic ladder and the examinations were more frequent. Yet to acquire the baccalaureate (equivalent to a BA) in the forties and fifties in pastoral Vietnam was something so rare that one's name was forever connected to one's title, as was the case with my paternal grandmother's closest friend, Ong Tu Tai Quoc—"Mr. Baccalaureate Quoc." Since so few made it to high school, to have a baccalaureate was to be assured of a bright future, and to be marked as very special, and rich families would offer their daughters' hands in marriage to the lucky laureate.

My paternal grandfather, who went to Faculty of Law in Bordeaux, came back and married my grandmother, daughter of one of the wealthiest men in the Mekong Delta. Father's three uncles on his mother's side were all French-educated. Our high family status back home, in many ways, was due to the level of education the men in Father's clan had achieved.

Over time, trudging toward higher education seemed to become embedded in the Vietnamese genes, a cultural value that lasted through war and peace and migration. For the Vietnamese immigrant to America, even if the insular world of family and clan has eroded by dispersion, the old penchant for learning remains intact. So far from home, we nevertheless worship at the temple of education.

America especially entices. The newcomers to this country find an array of colleges and universities to attract their scholastic souls. And if the competition is fierce, America, despite the naysayers and a shaky economy, remains the golden land of opportunities, especially compared to being stuck back home with little chance to advance.

For someone who was lucky enough to escape the horrors of Vietnam and be given ample opportunities in America to then abandon his potential seemed, therefore, something akin to a Confucian sin. By dislodging myself from my expected role within the family, I was, in a sense, being dishonorable. Or in a few relatives' description of me at the time: "selfish."

But such is the seduction of America. It summons betrayal of the parochial. America demands serious examination of the soul for children growing up between two conflicting cultures, two seeming antipodes, two opposed hemispheres. Asia will tell you to obey and honor parents' wishes, but America will tell you to look out for number one, to think for yourself. It whispers words of rebellion against the communal: Follow your dream...Take care of yourself first...You cannot make anyone else happy if you don't love yourself.

For children of Asian immigrants, to learn to negotiate between the "I" and the "We," between seemingly opposed ideas and flagrant contradictions, is in some way the most important lesson to learn, a skill much needed in order to appease and survive in both cultures.

This, then, was my secret desire: to stake a place in the world of literature. I was an inveterate bookworm. Until I left Vietnam I read French comic books and martial arts epics (translated from Chinese to Vietnamese) and even my mother's romance novels. Then, as if no major disruption had occurred despite my exile to America, I continued, reading American novels in my teen years, with a special affection for science fiction and fantasy and Buddhist texts. I spent my free time in the public libraries, devouring book after book each summer. When not studying, I could read a good novel in a single sleepless night.

I seriously doubt, were we still in Vietnam, even if the South had won the war and communism were in retreat, even if my family had retained our upper-class status, that I would have veered toward a self-directed path. If I mourned the loss of my homeland, I was also glad that I became an American. Here, perhaps like nowhere else, I was given the opportunity—as the mythologist Joseph Campbell would encourage you—to follow my bliss.

Back in my parents' living room, however, the argument went on. My parents wanted to know, if they could provide me with

$12,000 a year, would I consider perhaps, if med school was too difficult, dental school? My answer: No. This haggling went on for some time.

In the end I said good-bye to the old expectations, to familial demands, to the mice and the dreary labs, and off I went to creative writing school, and soon thereafter, a life in journalism, traveling and writing. Though there would be serious bouts of self-doubt, the quotidian aches and angst of the writing life, the insecurities, I'm happy to report that I haven't ever regretted my decision.

———

And yet that is not the whole story. The whole story belongs to romance, and the end of it, and the beginning of my writing life—which is to say, if I broke my parents' hearts all those years ago, I did so with a broken heart of my own.

In my freshman year at Berkeley I fell hopelessly in love; in the year after I graduated my heart shattered. While working at the cancer research laboratory on campus I took to writing, in part, in order to grieve. Daytime and I bombarded the mammary tissues of mice with various carcinogens to see how they grew; nights and I gave myself to memories, to heartbreak. I typed and typed. I got good at writing, bored with science, so I dropped the test tube and kept the proverbial pen.

Berkeley had indeed radicalized me. But I do not mean that in a political sense. No, the quiet, bookish, apolitical, obedient boy who didn't date in high school left his Vietnamese household and found sexual liberation in college, found carnal pleasure.

More important: I fell in love with "M." In "M's" embrace and kisses, what I had thought important until then turned out to be trivial. My desire to please my chronically unhappy mother was trivial, good grades were trivial, the path toward medical school, too, was trivial. "M," whose smile made me tremble, who was all there was, stole me away from my familial sense of duty. I found a new country, a new home.

What I remember, too, was an incident during my freshman year that, over time, marked me. A studious Chinese student tried to jump from the Campanile. He was from my dorm unit. He wanted to kill himself because, well, so went the gossip, he had never gotten a B before, until chemistry or some such difficult class overwhelmed him. I remember the entire dorm talking about it. I might have been momentarily horrified. But I was too busy being in love to let it really register. I do, however, remember thinking, and not without a certain vanity, that he *wouldn't* have considered jumping had he discovered love instead.

Other bubbles are coming up randomly now from under the deep dark waters of my college life: Professor Noyce in organic chemistry dragging on his thin cigarette, the smoke twirling in the air as he draws the nicotine molecules. "Don't ever smoke," he admonishes his audience. "It's bad for you." My roommate, Tony, who plays trumpet in the band, coming home from the big game, '82, crying with happiness. The Bears have just trampled the Stanford Band to score that spectacular and bizarre turnaround in the last seconds. I am walking down Telegraph Avenue at two in the morning and the street cleaner is spinning like some lazy grazing animal and the mist is rising at my feet. The bells of the Campanile ring out one humid afternoon and for no reason at all, I drop my backpack and, while spectators look on, dance.

Above all, though, the salty scent of "M."

Then "M" was gone. And my heart was broken.

Wasn't it then that I began to write? Wasn't it then that I began to bleed myself into words?

Yet it was not the larger world, nor my Vietnamese refugee experience, nor the Vietnam War that I wanted to address. I wrote about my unhappiness. I tried to capture what it was like to lose someone who had been my preoccupation throughout my college life; who was, in fact, my life then. Yet I was too close to the subject, too hurt to do the story justice. But the raw emotions unearthed another set of older memories simmering underneath. When one loses someone one loves, with whom one shares a private life, a private language, a private world, one loses an entire country, one becomes an exile.

But hadn't I been exiled before?

I had. The brokenhearted adult slowly found himself going back further, recalling the undressed wounds of the distraught child who stood alone on the beach of Guam, the camp with its khaki-green tents flapping in the wind, the child missing his friends, his dogs, fretting about his father, whose fate he had no way of knowing, and wondering if he'd ever see his homeland again.

My sadness opened a trapdoor to the past. A child forced to flee. The long line for food under a punishing sun. People weeping themselves to sleep. The family altar, where faded photographs of the dead stared out forlornly, the incense still burning but the living gone. A way of life stolen, a people scattered. I yearned for all my memories. I wrote some more. I began to go back.

Some years passed...

"These are Andrew Lam's awards," said my mother one afternoon to her friends when I was visiting and eavesdropping from upstairs. Sometimes my parents wouldn't say my Vietnamese name to their guests. "Andrew Lam" became someone else—related but somewhat remote, and yet important. For visitors, especially if it was their first visit, there would be an obligatory walk by the bookcase before sitting down for tea. On it were the various trophies and awards and diplomas, but chief among them, Andrew Lam's journalism awards.

"My son the Berkeley radical" became my father's favorite phrase when he introduced me to his friends. "Parents give birth to children, God gives birth to their personalities" became my mother's oft-repeated phrase, as a way to explain her youngest son. I don't take offense. I take it that this was their way of accepting how things can turn out in America, which is to say, unpredictable and heartbreaking.

I can't remember for sure how long he stood up there, or how he was talked down, that studious Chinese boy from the dorm. I do remember that around that time they put up metal bars on the Campanile so that no one else could jump.

Last year, after having revisited the Berkeley campus, where I was invited to give a talk about my writing life and about my various travels as a journalist, I had a dream. In it, it is me who finds himself atop the Campanile alone at sunset. I hesitate but I am not entirely afraid. I am not gripped by fear. Below, people are gathering. Before me: a beatific horizon. I leap. And soar high over the old campus before heading out to where sky kisses sea.

I haven't landed yet.

FROM RICE FIELDS TO MICROCHIPS:
THE VIETNAMESE STORY
IN CALIFORNIA

I am sitting in a small, comfortable bus going north, with the nostalgic music of Trinh Cong Son, sung by the raspy, smoky-voiced Khanh Ly, echoing from the overhead speaker. Son was the most famous Vietnamese composer during the Vietnam War, the master of existential love songs, and Khanh Ly the most famous singer. Two old Vietnamese ladies next to me are bragging about their children and grandchildren, how well they are doing and so on. Behind me, a couple of middle-aged men hum along with the song of their youth. Up front, two kids are playing handheld computer games while their mother talks endlessly on her cell phone to someone about her restaurant business.

Vietnamese voices rise and fall; I close my eyes, listen. I swear, I could be heading north to Nha Trang or Da Nang from Saigon.

Except, I am not. I am on the other side of the Pacific, on my way to San Jose from Orange County, going up Highway 5 in a bus owned by one of two competing Vietnamese companies.

I am telling you about this at the beginning of an essay about the Vietnamese in California because I find it to be one of the major lifelines that connect the various Little Saigons at the turn of the millennium. Brand-new and much more comfortable than your regular Greyhound—they even give you a Vietnamese-style sandwich for lunch and a soybean drink—it connects the various

Vietnamese communities in California and beyond (and yes, you can go from Orange County on a Vietnamese-owned bus to Las Vegas, where there's a growing Vietnamese population). And it is telling, in terms of how far we've come as a community since the first wave of refugees arrived in 1975 at the end of the Vietnam War, a huddled mass wearing donated clothes, frantically looking for homes, for jobs.

In *Tribes*, author Joel Kotkin defines a quintessentially cosmopolitan global tribe as an international community which combines a strong sense of a common origin with "two critical factors for success in the modern world: geographic dispersion and a belief in scientific progress." Kotkin's primary examples include the British, Jews, Chinese, Japanese, and Indians. These groups, relying on mutual dependence and trust, have created global networks that allow them "to function collectively beyond the confines of national or regional borders."

In later writings, Kotkin added Vietnamese to the list.

More than four million Vietnamese have fled or migrated abroad. They are scattered onto five different continents and have reestablished themselves everywhere. These days you can find Vietnamese restaurants all the way to South Africa, Brazil, and Israel. I myself have relatives living in six different countries and on three continents. But almost half of the diaspora ended up in North America, and the largest portion of that population resettled in California.

Why California? It was a matter of luck, initially. Camp Pendleton, a Marine Corps base near San Diego, accommodated the bulk of the first wave of Vietnamese refugees; Pendleton was our own Ellis Island, as it were. Tony Bui, a Vietnamese American filmmaker raised in San Jose, California, made *Green Dragon* as a tribute to the Vietnamese Americans' beginnings, and it was the story of refugee life in Camp Pendleton circa 1975. Slowly, many generous, caring Americans sponsored them out of the camp.

The bulk resettled in nearby Orange County, Los Angeles, and San Diego County. Others moved up north, to the Bay Area, and then, later on, to the San Joaquin Valley. To put it succinctly, California, though at first reluctant, eventually welcomed Vietnamese asylum seekers, and they, in turn, embraced the Golden State.

Many of those who initially ended up in other states made a second migration here, to join their relatives, to escape the cold weather elsewhere, and to find jobs. Others, boat people, immigrants, Vietnamese living in Europe and Asia, made their way to California as well, sponsored and beckoned by their Californian relatives, all hoping to strike it rich.

Numbering around one million in the U.S., more than half a million Vietnamese Americans are living in California, giving the state the distinction of having the largest population of Vietnamese outside of Vietnam. They are nowhere near as wealthy or connected as Kotkin's long-established prime examples, but their trajectory increasingly fits his description of a global tribe.

Those sunburnt, scrawny people holding their SOS signs on the crowded boats seen on American television in the late seventies and early eighties have transformed into a vibrant ethnic group in America.

How vibrant? The *San Jose Mercury News* had a study done in the late nineties and found that "Santa Clara County's Vietnamese community is a major market, with an estimated buying power of $1.8 billion. Vietnamese represent 6% of Santa Clara County's total population [around 100,000]—a higher percentage than any other market in the nation. Growing in size and buying power, this is a valuable audience for any advertiser." So much so that the *Mercury News* was among the first mainstream papers to have a Vietnamese language weekly to compete with the various Vietnamese-owned media.

Or consider politics: a whopping eighteen Vietnamese American candidates ran for office in California in 2006, even if only three won. That's an unprecedented number for a three-decade-old community whose history was defined by its initial immigration to America as refugees. There's a Vietnamese American state assemblyman. There's a Vietnamese American mayor of Rosemead, California. There's a Vietnamese American member of the Orange County Board of Supervisors. A new member of Congress, Joseph Cao (Rep.-New Orleans), is a rising star (though, alas, he's not from California).

Recently, a Vietnamese-language newspaper in San Jose called *Calitoday* reported on the subject of Little Saigon and American elections. A picture on its front page showed Vietnamese gathering in large numbers on Bolsa Avenue in Orange County. But they were not protesting against communism, which is a communal trademark of various Vietnamese communities in the U.S. They came out to listen to candidates speak and to encourage others to vote. A few were holding up signs. One said, "Our voice is our vote." My favorite, however, is the one borrowed from the immigration rights movement. It said, "Today we rally, tomorrow we vote."

EXILE TO IMMIGRANT

Ours is an epic filled with irony: traumatized by wars, bound by old ways of life where land and ancestors are worshipped, where babies' umbilical cords are buried as a way to spiritually bind them to our ancient land, we nevertheless relocated to a state created by fabulous fantasies, high-tech wizardry, and individual ambitions. You only need to contrast Trinh Cong Son's antiwar song "Mother's Inheritance" to the sophistication of the bus—it comes complete with a TV set playing all sorts of Vietnamese music videos and kung fu movies, and the aforementioned kids and their mothers, with their video games and cell phones.

One of the two old ladies next to me comments that she cannot get over the fact that her son and her grandchildren live in a big house on a hill in Fremont. "To think my son, back home, wore shorts and played in the rice field, and all my kids studied by lamp-light. Now he's a big-shot engineer. It's so different, our lives, all these machines," she says, and looks out to the verdant knolls that blur pass us. Then instead of being relieved, she sighs and says in a voice full of nostalgia, "We've come so far from home."

Personally, when I think of Vietnamese narrative in Califor-nia I think of my mother's ancestral altar. In her suburban home on the outskirts of San Jose, she climbs a chair every morning, lights some incense for the ancestral altar, and says her prayers to the dead. Black-and-white photos of Grandpa and Grandma and uncles stare out benevolently to the world of the living on the top shelf. On the shelves below, by contrast, stand my father's MBA, my older siblings' engineering and business degrees, my own degree in biochemistry, our combined sports trophies, and, last but not least, the latest installments in my own unending quest for self-reinvention—plaques and obelisks, shaped crystals and framed certificates—my journalism and writing awards.

What mother's altar and the shelves carrying their various knickknacks underneath seek to tell is the story of the Viet-namese American transition, one in which Old World fatalism finally meets New World optimism, the American dream. After all, praying to the dead is a cyclical, Confucian habit—one looks to the past for guidance, and one yearns toward that "common origin" that Kotkin talked about, to keep oneself connected to community, to a sense of self. Getting awards and trophies, on the other hand, is an American tendency, a proposition of ascen-dancy, where one looks toward the future and deems it optimistic and bright. To be Vietnamese American is to lurk between these two opposite ideas, negotiating, that is, between night and day.

Many Vietnamese American immigrants, when they talk about their own lives, will tell you how drastically different they were before and after they left Vietnam. "Before I left, I couldn't possibly imagine what my life in America would be like." This sentence, or some version of it, I often hear from my relatives and friends when they talk about the past.

Day and night. In the dead of night, bent on an American conversion, thousands climbed aboard old rickety boats and headed for America. "Going to America," so goes the new Vietnamese mantra, "is like going to heaven." America is where reincarnation can be had in one lifetime. Go to America and your sufferings end. Go to America and your sons and daughters will grow up to be astronauts or presidents of rich computer companies.

Night and day. Under the cerulean sky of California the newcomers undergo the golden transformation. Sean Nguyen, for instance, was once a rice farmer. When the war ended he fled with his father and brother to America, where he worked in a factory assembling modems and studied English at night. Then he ran a family-owned multimillion-dollar corporation assembling computer circuit boards. In the mid-nineties he returned to Vietnam several times to open a factory in the province where he once lived. In 1993 President Clinton named him Young Entrepreneur of the Year.

What transformed the Vietnamese psyche was a simple yet potent idea of progression. In the Golden State, where dreams do have a penchant for coming true, one grows ambitious. He sees his kids graduating from top colleges. He imagines his own home with a pool in the back in five years' time—all things that were impossible back home.

The drama of the initial expulsion is replaced over the years by the jubilation of newfound status and wealth. A community that initially saw itself as living in exile, as survivors of some historical blight, slowly changed its self-assessment. It began to see itself as an immigrant community. And immigrants' strong work ethic built the American dream, which in turn merges with the old Protestant work ethic, which built America. To have vision is to move forward: he sees in the boarded-up store a sparkling new restaurant; she looks at the pile of shirts to be sewn in the sweat-shop and sees her children going to Harvard. For those who want to do well, America is still the place to be.

Pick up the Vietnamese yellow pages in Santa Clara or Orange County these days and you will be astounded at how organized the community really is. The new arrival may not need to speak English at all (though of course, he should learn it)—he just needs that phone book full of businesses that cater to an immi-grant's every need: from lawyers to dentists, from restaurants to computer programming training centers, from private schools to rental cars to realtors, from funeral services to wedding planning, from temples to churches, from cosmetic surgery to travel agents, he has an array of choices at his beck and call. Even when the economy is shaky, ours is a community that continues to thrive, providing that much-needed safety net in an age of foreclosure and failing banks.

"It's a who-you-know economy," explains Chanh Pham, who organizes annual Vietnamese fashion shows and beauty contests in the Bay Area and designs modern Vietnamese *ao dai* dresses. He says that community-owned services are crucial to his success. "Vietnamese services are more convenient and a lot cheaper. I use a Vietnamese printing press in Orange County for my calendars and posters because it's good and cheap, then I get them delivered to San Francisco by using the Vietnamese bus service. It's about fifteen times cheaper than Fed Ex."

Competition also helps drives down prices, Pham says. "Some-times we underestimate the power of small businesses that thrive due to cheap labor and high volumes."

Take Lee's sandwiches. Its baguette sandwiches are sold for less than three dollars, and while the profit margins may be low, the sheer volumes have made its owner very rich. Chieu Le escaped by boat in 1979 from Vietnam, added an *e* to his last name for easy pronunciation, started out with a catering truck that parked outside electronic assembly plants in San Jose selling sandwiches to mostly Vietnamese workers, and parlayed that business into a multimillion-dollar chain. There are now twenty-two Lee's Sandwiches shops in California, Arizona, and Texas, and Chieu Le's second business, Lee's Catering, has five hundred trucks delivering cooked food every day.

VIETNAM AND THE AMERICAN CONVERSATION

Back home, until recent times, Vietnam's narrative of herself was that she's four thousand years old, her milk is dry, her hair gray, and she suffers from astigmatism. She has little to offer her numerous children. America, on the other hand, is young, rich, optimistic: everything that Vietnam cannot be. Vietnamese, increasingly younger and full of yearnings, inevitably dream of America, a place they imagine of peace, freedom, wealth, and little suffering.

For let it be noted that despite the horror and bloodshed, the Vietnamese missed the Americans after they abandoned the country. A particular story of boat people in the news in the early nineties still resonates in my mind: a dilapidated boat carrying refugees drifted into Malaysian waters, displaying on the side of the vessel a peculiar sign that read: "USA REMAINS ON MY BOAT."

Bones. American bones, which once lay buried in tropical graves, have been unearthed, washed, and carefully wrapped by impoverished hands. Then when they flee their homeland, refugees carry the bones with them. Malaysia had a malicious practice of pushing these boats back out. But the refugees were hoping that the bones could serve as talismans or passports to barter their way to the Promised Land.

That sign on the boat said more than it intended to. Stepping over broken wings of warplanes and moss-covered fragments of rusty old tanks, young Vietnamese search for America. The

American relics offer a wondrous possibility. Assemble the broken parts and you might end up with a car, a bridge, or even a homemade factory. Dig up some missing bones and crown the assemblage with an MIA's dog tags and, who knows, you might turn it into a coveted treasure.

And who can blame them? The rich, well-fed Vietnamese American tourists return to Vietnam praising America. The impoverished cousins at home notice that their relatives carry with them a certain foreign air, exuding glamour. "They are boasters and braggarts," one cousin complained to our family in the early nineties in a letter about his younger sibling, who had left two decades earlier. "They walk faster, speak louder, and smell different and take up more space."

With their Gucci bags and Giorgio Armani suits, the returning visitors pull out snapshots of their children in the United States. "See, Tree Hang and Hien? They're Helen and Henry now. Aren't they so tall? It's the American milk and peanut butter, you know. They make your bones large and strong. Henry has a PhD. And Aunty, look..."

The relatives devour the photographs with hungry eyes. Beyond those handsome, smiling young adults who pose with such ease next to their sleek sports cars stands, inevitably, that elegant two-story house with its two-car garage, as if in mockery. In the eighties and early nineties, like sirens, such images became the final call for boat people, luring them from their shantytowns toward the open sea.

After the Cold War ended, Vietnamese refugees were no longer welcome in the West, and as forced repatriation became more or less a new international policy, boat people stopped coming. But the migration did not stop. It continues to this day, albeit in a more orderly way. Relatives sponsor relatives, Vietnamese marry Vietnamese Americans, political and religious prisoners and Vietnamese Amerasians come under U.S. special programs, and the latest wave, well-to-do and bright Vietnamese foreign students, apply to study in the U.S. All are hopeful for a golden transformation.

So much yearning for America changes the character of Vietnam itself. *Vuot bien*, "to cross the border," for instance, became a household verb in Vietnam in the eighties. *Viet Kieu* literally means Vietnamese nationals living abroad—a powerful symbol in the nineties. And it is universally understood that the Viet Kieu, with their wealth and influence, can change the fortunes of their poor cousins back home.

Many Viet Kieu have returned to visit, work, live, invest, and retire in Vietnam. Hanoi is even considering granting dual citizenship to Viet Kieu to spur further repatriation. In the wake of that bitter civil war is an irony: those persecuted by Uncle Ho's followers and forced to flee abroad are now being actively solicited to return to Vietnam to help rebuild and invest in the government that once spurned them.

Some economists will argue that the remittances Vietnamese living abroad sent home helped Vietnam's economy stay afloat during the Cold War, when the U.S. imposed economic sanctions on the country for occupying Cambodia. In fact, remittances have continued unabated since then, growing 10 to 15 percent annually. Despite the worldwide economic downturn, Vietnamese abroad annually send home some $7.5 billion, making an enormous contribution to the country's economic development.

But the overseas influence on Vietnam is far more than remittances. It is profound. For if it was once generally understood that a Vietnamese soul is tied to home and hearth, in the last three decades that old land-bound assumption has been radically subverted by the Viet Kieu.

So much so that a new and radical idea has injected itself into the Vietnamese land-bound imagination. It is a powerful migratory myth, one that extolls fabulous, glamorous endings. It is not an exaggeration to say our successes and transformation have subverted the language of nationalism in our homeland. "I have a relative in California" is a common boast that Vietnamese in Saigon will share with me when I visit and tell them where I am from. I still have the photo of that first trip back to Vietnam in 1991: the first fast food joint selling hamburgers opened in Saigon, its large billboard painted with these words in red: "Ca Li Pho Nha."

TECHNOLOGY, COMMUNITY, AND MEMORIES

The subject line: "Looking for old acquaintance." The body, in broken English:

> *Is this email of Mr. Andrew Lam? I was private math teacher of your family at the time before 04-30-1975 in Saigon. I had been taught Mr Lam Quang Tuan, Ms Lam thi bich Ngoc, and you. Though this email is exactly or not, answer me some words please! Hope for more tale!*
> *—Mr Phan Kim Anh, Da Nang, Vietnam*

Long out of touch, the math tutor has found me and my siblings through the Internet. Upon reading his email I am a child again, listening to Brother Anh going on and on about the importance of math. A gentle young man with a ready smile, he, like so many others, was lost to us when the end of the war sent us scattering. But if war and migration separated us, technology renewed otherwise impossible ties.

Not so long ago, the ocean was vast, homesickness was an incurable malady, and a Vietnamese overseas had little more than nostalgic memories to keep cultural ties alive. There was a time when leaving meant risking one's life in the turbulent sea, and one who did make it to foreign shores would not expect to ever see the homeland again.

These days, long after the Cold War melted, Vietnam is but an eighteen-hour flight from California, and Vietnamese and

Vietnamese Americans chat online, text one another, talk on Skype, talk on cell phones, and follow on Internet websites the latest trends and news from home. The camcorder shows Grandma back home what life is like in America, and the Internet connects all across the globe, shrinking the once vast ocean to the size of a pond.

On YouTube, singers from the distant past reappear in old videos, singing songs I haven't heard in decades. School pals from my old grade school in Saigon form an alumni association in San Jose, inviting our fifth grade teacher over from Australia for a reunion. Long lost relatives are found again, friends and neighbors are reacquainted, thanks largely to technology.

"The information age is far more important to Vietnamese than the industrial revolution," Nam Nguyen, editor-in-chief of *Calitoday*, told me. Nguyen and his wife and two kids escaped Vietnam by boat, came to the U.S. in the mid-eighties. Now the entire family works on the newspaper, whose office is the size of a large living room, with half a dozen computers humming all day long. Yet it has readers from San Jose to San Francisco to Sacramento and many more online. Like other mom-and-pop media outlets, the Nguyens' newspaper survives solely on advertising. They will tell you they have benefited greatly from easy desktop publishing software and affordable computers and printing presses. In San Jose alone, there are seven Vietnamese-language magazines and weeklies, two daily newspapers, one television program, and two radio shows. And in Orange County, you can easily multiply all that by three. Vietnamese call Silicon Valley "Valley of Gold Flowers." This is because we, perhaps more than any other new immigrant group in California, have benefited from the high-tech boom.

So while some native-born Americans may blame technology— the ATM, the automated gas pump, the Home Shopping Network, the Internet—for breaking down community and family ties, many Asian immigrants will tell you it has had the reverse effect on their lives. With the advent of communication technology, Vietnamese living today can generate and disseminate their own media, their own history, information that's close to their hearts.

When I graduated from the University of California, Berkeley, in the late eighties, almost three out of four of my Vietnamese peers were graduating with engineering degrees. Many ended up in Silicon Valley, others went to Southern California to work. It is no surprise, then, that one of a handful of Vietnamese *ca dao*—or adages—coined abroad praises the good life in Silicon Valley. *"Chong tach, vo li, di lam cung xep, con gi xuong hon?"*— Husband technician, wife in assembly line, working on the same shift, is there anything better?

One electronics engineer in Silicon Valley told me he visited Vietnamese communities all over the U.S., trying to encourage small companies and businesses to get online: "These communities are doing very well. And as a people, we are using the Internet more and more to communicate, and to do commerce and grow."

So while other global tribes may have a strong "belief in scientific progress," as Kotkin would put it, here in California, Vietnamese immigrants have turned this belief into a kind of religion, and it's most evident in Silicon Valley. Professor Chung Chuong, who teaches Vietnamese American studies at San Francisco City College, once told me that "Vietnamese have greatly benefited from the high-tech boom since the early eighties. It's not a mistake that the second-largest Vietnamese population in the U.S. is situated in Santa Clara County."

For an immigrant population with low language skills but a strong desire to move ahead, the best route is to become technicians. "Back in the eighties, you could get trained for less than six months and make enough money working overtime to buy a house after a few years," observed professor Chuong.

Nam Nguyen readily agreed with that assessment. "The strategy doesn't end there, of course. The adults tell our kids to study and study hard—the sciences, especially. One of the strongest of Vietnamese cultural characteristics is that we put education above all else. In California many Vietnamese end up working both on the lower and upper tier of the high-tech industry." And it only follows that we would in time start our own companies, reinvest in Vietnam, and outsource to our homeland, he said.

Once, I visited a friend with a PhD in computer engineering from MIT who designed microchips for a living. But in his off-hours he wrote software for *Tu Vi*—Vietnamese-Chinese horoscopes based on complex astrology. He told me there is no contradiction between his daytime occupation and nighttime passion. In fact to him, and to many Vietnamese immigrants in America, they mesh.

"Technology is just a tool," my friend the horoscope reader said. "It's up to you to bring your passions and interests to it. It can pay your bills or it can store your cultural traditions and memories." He held up a microchip the size of the tiniest teardrop in which the program for horoscopes and all of its mysticism is installed. I leaned down and looked. Under the lamplight, and through the magnifying glass, the microchip with its tiny grids that store parochial memories resembled the rice field writ very, very small.

AT A CROSSROAD: THE PAST, THE PRESENT, THE FUTURE

The reason I am on this bus is this: I went to Orange County to see for myself the Vietnam War Memorial that I heard so much about from my parents. My father, once a high-ranking South Vietnamese officer, was on the advisory committee of this memorial-building endeavor. Within one evening, Vietnamese in Orange County raised more than $200,000 for the memorial. Well-known Vietnamese singers sang for free and ticket receipts all went to fund-raising for the memorial. A decade in the making, with lobbying efforts that showed both political savvy and determination, the memorial was two life-size statues, one a South Vietnamese, the other an American GI, standing side by side in combat fatigues adjacent to the city hall in Westminster.

Standing in front of it, I was of two opposed minds. I felt something akin to patriotism for my long lost homeland restirred in my blood, and a deep sadness for the men who fought and died and those who survived broken; I felt, at the same time, a dire need for distance. While I stood there on a Saturday evening, a couple of older women lit incense and prayed and several older Vietnamese men in army uniforms stood guard nearby. Something somber and heavy in their stance suggested a collective sorrow that caused me to shudder; their eyes—eyes that no doubt saw the worst of the old war—conveyed anger, hatred, and bitterness. Their faces, inevitably, reminded me of my father's.

It occurred to me then that while one strand of history still defines those men in army uniforms and, of course, my father, another strand of history was redefining me. My father considers himself an exile living in America, part of an increasingly small population; I see myself as an American journalist who happens to make many journeys to Vietnam without much emotional fanfare. For me, Vietnam, my country of birth, and its tumultuous history have become a point of departure, an occasional destination and concern, but no longer home. The irony is that because he holds Vietnam so dear to his heart, my father cannot return to the country to which he owes allegiance, so long as the current regime remains in power. His is a rage left over from the Cold War that has no end in sight. History, for my father and for those men who still wear their army uniforms at every communal event, has a tendency to run backwards, to memories of the war, to a bitter and bloody struggle whose end spelled their defeat and exile. And it holds them static in a lonely nationalist stance. They live in America but their souls are still fighting an unfinished war in Vietnam.

But if they seek to isolate Vietnam, it is too late. Vietnam, despite its human rights violations, has for a while now been a member of the World Trade Organization, has integrated rapidly into the world economy and can no longer be isolated. Instead, over time, the business of regime change has turned into the business of keeping Little Saigon from changing, and the bulk of these efforts is in the realm of the symbolic: flying the flags of South Vietnam in shopping malls, erecting war memorials for fallen soldiers, and, lately, fighting over the names of business districts—actions that have no apparent effect on Vietnam itself.

The old passion lives on, but it must now contend with the new integration: the Vietnamese diaspora, no longer in exile, is steadily moving back into Vietnam's orbit. Lan Nguyen, writing for *Nguoi Viet*, the largest Vietnamese paper in Orange County, noted that "While the younger generation of Vietnamese Americans shares with elders a general concern regarding human rights, democracy, and freedom in Vietnam, they are not as invested in the cause." Nguyen, who lives in San Jose, cites language barriers and lack of experience under communism as the factors that help widen the generation gap. "The Vietnamese American youth... often are disillusioned as it seems their every effort to help Vietnam is met with criticism by those older than them. The elders in turn are horrified to see young people organize philanthropic missions to Vietnam."

The question is whether the Vietnamese diaspora can be an effective agent of change and find new ways to influence the future of the country. To do so, it needs to ask tough questions. Is there real freedom for those who give in to their hatred and are ruled by it? Is democracy for Vietnam possible when those who live in America often fail to understand and practice it, and the majority of those in Vietnam barely show any interest? And what does it take to move beyond anger and lust for revenge, and create space for constructive discussion and dialogue and spur new political thoughts?

It is true: once the hate is gone, in its place is pain. Those who cling so strongly to hatred, I suspect, are often those who fear what's after it. But it is true also that many of us have moved on beyond the old rancor, beyond that us-versus-them mentality. We have learned to absorb our pain and grief and are negotiating our positions between East and West, memories and modernity, traditions and individual ambitions, old loyalty and new alliances, such that we are in the process of recreating a whole notion of what it means to be Vietnamese, a definition that is both open-ended and inclusive.

A friend of mine from Los Angeles lost siblings to Thai pirates when they escaped from Vietnam. She returned to Saigon, where she is now a thriving entrepreneur. "My success is the best revenge," she once told me. Another, the son of a colonel who spent fourteen years in re-education, spent his honeymoon in Vietnam despite his dislike of the Hanoi regime. A friend who was forced to escape as a boat person returned with money raised in Silicon Valley to create a foundation to help families who might otherwise sell their children to traffickers in the Mekong Delta. Another has gone back to help build schools in the rural areas.

It is a worthy goal, after all, is to move beyond hatred or resentment and find the resilience with which to deal with the tragedies one has experienced personally. Having been victims of the war, these people have emerged as victors of the peace. They've managed to remake themselves and go on with their lives, and more important, by refusing to let rage and thirst for vengeance dominate their hearts, some have become active agents in changing the destiny of Vietnam itself.

NEW MYTH

Nam Nguyen said that the Vietnamese myth of the birth of their nation should be revised. It's a story all Vietnamese schoolchildren learn. In an ancient time, a dragon married a fairy and they gave birth to one hundred eggs. The eggs hatched and became the Vietnamese people. A new Vietnamese is being "hatched" abroad, Nguyen says, beyond the homeland, free of vehemence, and a new myth is needed. "Who he is nobody knows, for he is not yet described in any Vietnamese myths or literature."

But I've seen him. He's Brandon, my little nephew, surfing the web while his grandparents watch Chinese martial arts videos dubbed in Vietnamese. Nearby is the ancestral altar from which faded images of the dead stare with forlorn eyes into a new world. On the computer screen, images of a Japanese video game shift and flow. Brandon is very much at home with all these conflicting ideas, dissimilar languages and sensibilities. Ask him what he wants to be when he grows up and he distractedly shrugs. "A fireman. A martial arts master. Or, maybe an astronaut!"

Go back three generations and he might still stand knee-deep in mud in the rice fields, gawking at the moon and stars. But no more. His energy is free from the grip of land-bound imagination. For Brandon, who knows? The moon and stars may very well be possible. May he remember and appreciate his inheritance, but may his heart be freed of the old rancor and historical vehemence. And may he be inspired by the communal but otherwise be self-directed. And may he inherit many additional homelands and languages as he travels far and wide beyond the Golden State.

WHO WILL LIGHT INCENSE?

She turns seventy but she remains a vivacious woman—her hair is still mostly black, there is still a girlish twang in her laughter, and her eyes twinkle at the telling of a joke—still, mortality weighs heavily on her soul. After the gifts are opened and the cake eaten, Mother whispers to her younger sister-in-law: "Who will light incense to the dead when I'm gone?"

Aunty shakes her head. "Honestly, I don't know. None of my children will do it, and we can forget the grandchildren. They don't even understand what we are doing when we pray to the dead. I guess when we're gone, the ritual ends."

Such is the price of living in America. I myself can't remember the last time I lit incense sticks and talked to my dead ancestors. Having fled so far from Vietnam, I can no longer imagine what to say, or how I should address my prayers, or for that matter what promises I could possibly make to the long departed.

My mother, on the other hand, lives in America the way she would in Vietnam. Every morning in my parents' suburban home north of San Jose, with a pool shimmering in the backyard, she climbs a chair and piously lights a few joss sticks for the ancestral altar, which sits on top of the living room's bookcase. Every morning she talks to ghosts.

She mumbles solemn prayers to the spirits of our dead ancestors, and to the all-compassionate Buddha. What is she asking for? Protection for her children and grandchildren, and that they should prosper in America.

At that far end of the Asian immigrant narrative, however, I will readily admit that I cannot help but feel a certain twinge of guilt and regret upon hearing my mother's question to Aunty. Once upon a time, in that other world, I was a pious child. I paid obeisance to the dead, prayed for good health. As the youngest in my family, it was my task to climb the table over which the altar stood. It was I who placed the incense in the bronze urn nightly.

In America, however, I became rebellious, distant. And once Mother asked me to speak more Vietnamese inside the house. "No," I answered in English, curtly. "What good is it to speak it, Mom? It's not as if I'm going to use it after I move out."

She had this pained look in her eyes. If she was proud of his accomplishments, she mourned the distance that had grown between her and her youngest son. Something in the water, in the airwaves, changed his inner makeup and dulled his Confucian ways. America gave him too much freedom. America made him self-centered, introspective. "He thinks too hard, he reads too much," she complained to Father, who shook his head and smiled.

We have made peace since then, she and I, but it does not mean that I have become a traditional, incense-lighting Vietnamese son. I visit. I take her to lunch. I come home for important dates— New Year, Thanksgiving, Tet, grandfather's death anniversary.

But these days, in front of the family altar with all those faded photos of the dead staring down at me, I often feel oddly removed, as if staring not at the present, but a relic of my distant past. And when, upon my mother's insistence, I light incense, I do not feel as if I am participating in a living tradition so much as pleasing my traditional mother.

We live in two different worlds, after all, she and I. Mine is a world of travel and writing and public speaking; hers is a world of consulting the Vietnamese horoscope and eating vegetarian food when the moon is full, of attending Buddhist temple on the day of her parents' death anniversaries, a pious devotion.

But at her birthday party, having listened to her worries, I had to wonder: what will indeed survive, Mother?

I wish I could say that I will pick it up as naturally as any Vietnamese in Vietnam would. I wish I could assure her that, after she is gone, each morning I will light incense for her and all the ancestors' spirits before her, but I can't.

Yet, if some rituals die, some others have only just begun. I am, after all, not a complete American brat, dear mother. Every morning I write, rendering memories into words. I write, going back further, invoking the past precisely because it is irretrievable. I write if only, in the end, to take leave.

And this morning, with the San Francisco fog drifting outside my window, it occurs to me as I type these words that this too, strangely enough, is a kind of ritual, a kind of filial impulse to reconcile Mother's world and my own. The solemnity of the act—my fingers gliding on the keyboard, my mind on things ethereal—is something akin, at last, to my mother's morning prayers.

MOURNING THE LOSS OF THE TIGER

When I was six or seven, a frail and asthmatic child living in cool and foggy Dalat, Vietnam, my great-aunt gave me a broth made of tiger bone. She promised it would turn me into a robust child. My mother, a great believer in ancient remedies, readily consented.

"You are lucky," Great-aunt told me as she poured the steaming black broth into a bowl. "With all the bombings, there aren't that many tigers left in our country. You, boy, might be drinking the bones of the last one."

I watched the soup billowing smoke in front of me and felt as if I was about to swallow poison. To make things worse, the tiger was my favorite animal and I felt wholly unworthy to receive such a sacrifice. But a Vietnamese child is obedient; I wept, but I drank.

The broth was full of herbal smell, its bitter taste suggesting a thousand wiggly jungle things. Half a dozen bowls of tiger-bone soup followed over the next few weeks, but I continued to wheeze and heave and cough. Then Great-aunt ran out of tiger bone and the treatment mercifully ended.

After I reached puberty in America, my asthma went away and I grew robust. But a different kind of malady remains to this day, made up of guilt and the feeling that my fate is somehow intertwined with the fate of the tiger.

There are fewer than six thousand tigers still living in the wild, worldwide—most of them in South Asia and disappearing fast due to encroachment and poachers—and I have this strange, if unreasonable, feeling that when the last one goes, maybe so will I.

Perhaps it came the moment the dark broth passed my lips, or because I was born in the Vietnamese year of the cat (equivalent to the Chinese rabbit). Perhaps it has to do with the hundreds of stories I heard as a child about long ago, when the Vietnamese people lived at the edge of an immense jungle, where a tiger ruled. Country people in fact often call the tiger "Grandfather" rather than use its proper name, for many believe their ancestors' spirits sometimes take residence in wild animals.

Our old houseman, Uncle Cam, claimed the peculiar bald spot on the side of his head was "a gift from Grandfather." As a teenager, he told us, he often went foraging in the forest near Hue, the imperial city, and one day he crossed paths with a fierce tiger. Uncle Cam dropped to his knees, threw away his axe, and begged for his life. Moved by his eloquence, the tiger spared him and marked him as a relative (not to be eaten by other tigers) by licking the side of his head. Uncle Cam's hair promptly fell out, and it never grew back.

Even if I grew to doubt his story, I nevertheless felt a sense of camaraderie with the old man. Both of us, I felt, were deeply marked by the ruler of the dark jungle and would live beholden to his spirit and generosity. Of course this sentiment is neither rational nor logical, but neither is the human relationship with wild beasts. Indeed, it is primitive and full of superstition—we burden wild animals with all sorts of human characteristics and fantasies, and we slay them because we covet or fear what we think they represent. The lion is courageous, the snake evil, the owl wise, the rhino sturdy and invulnerable, the fox cunning, and the tiger—the tiger, above all—is majestic, elegant, full of prowess and grace. It inspires awe.

Alas, the tiger's grip on our imagination is precisely the force that drives it toward extinction. The region where the great cats once roamed is no longer one of dark jungles and steppes and folklore. Forests have been logged, slashed and burned, and many wild animals poached to near extinction. Soon, I suspect, there will be nothing to fear "in the wild" anymore because there will be no more "wild" anywhere.

The only wilderness left is within; human beings have conquered everything but ourselves. We have decided, in the age of global warming, that we are our greatest enemy, our own stalker, and ultimately, our own destroyer. We consume all that lies in our path.

In Vietnam, one third of Vietnamese depend solely on the forest and forest products for their living, and the number is rising steadily, according to the United Nations Development Program. Whereas the entire Vietnam War destroyed close to five million acres of forestland, almost fifty million more have been destroyed because of population pressures since the war ended more than three decades ago.

The way things are going, I doubt I will ever run across a tiger the way Uncle Cam did, except in its many parts: that "fearful symmetry" that William Blake immortalized in his poem is now reduced to skin, bones, and dried penis, made into balms, soaked in wines, and ground into pills, and sold at specialty shops in Hong Kong, Bangkok, and Beijing.

Not long ago Vietnamese, unlike westerners, viewed people as inseparable from nature. They taught their children to revere the spirits that protected forests and rivers and often named their children after forest animals. Buddhist temples were places of worship and for learning the ecological balance between man and nature.

My great-aunt was a good-hearted woman but she was not sentimental about tigers—if the last one went, well, it was a matter of good fortune that its bones should help her precious nephew. Alas, I fear hers is a popular sentiment that hasn't changed much despite the advent of much more effective Western medicines, such as Viagra as an aphrodisiac, Propecia for hair growth, and so on. If anything, the rarer the remedy, the higher the demand. Mass consumerism in Asia coupled with deforestation spells disaster for the tiger and, of course, for the rest of wildlife.

A while back at a Buddhist temple in Hong Kong, I saw a little boy tracing a bas relief of exquisitely carved dragons and tigers with his fingers. "Mama," he asked, "does the tiger really exist, or is it just like the dragon?"

His mother answered with a sigh. "It is still real, but maybe not for very much longer."

"How come?" he asked.

But the boy's mother just shrugged.

I knew the answer, of course. I, and the others, have swallowed it, and try as I may to regurgitate, all there is left of that poor, beautiful beast is a bitter aftertaste.

SINGING IN THE FAMILY

On the recent occasion of my uncle's sixtieth birthday, my mother's clan gathered from all over the country to celebrate at my brother's home in Fremont, California. Instead of gifts, however, my uncle, the youngest of seven siblings, had an unusual wish: everyone was asked to pick and sing a song on the karaoke machine.

What began as an amusing exercise in merriment turned quickly into something I can only describe as our first and only session in family group therapy.

When it comes to matters close to the heart, my family, like so many others from Vietnam, is notoriously inexpressive. Something within our taciturn culture discourages verbal intimacy. Immigrants and refugees from Vietnam, we rarely ever communicate to one another what we really feel; our love and resentments are all hidden, our losses and sorrows often digested differently and alone.

My uncle, who was going through a painful divorce, had not been able to convey to the family his profound sadness. He was still in love with his wife, but he was traumatized by memories of the war, in which he took part as a pilot, and prone to bouts of rage and mania and ranting: she had had it with him. He masked this with jokes and once said, while drunk, "Vietnamese men don't cry outward. Our tears flow inward, back into the heart."

But at the birthday bash we all discovered that what we could not talk about, some of us could at least sing out loud.

Thus the cousin whose wife had filed for a divorce sang Tom Jones's "Delilah" with a heartbreaking voice. And we managed to tell him that we were sorry for his troubles by singing along with every refrain, "My, my, my Delilah! Why, why, why, Delilah?"

Another aunt, not particularly well liked for her condescending attitudes over the years but who now was in declining health, took the mike to sing, rather breathlessly, "Somewhere My Love," the theme song from the 1960s film *Doctor Zhivago*, dedicating it to the rest of us. "Till then, my sweet, think of me now and then," she sang in a hoarse whisper and out of tune. "Godspeed my love, till you are mine again." A few of us cried quiet tears as we listened to that thin and frail woman sing gamely on. Her life had not been easy, for she, too, was abandoned by her husband when her children were young.

After a few more singers, it was Uncle's turn. He chose a well-known Vietnamese song titled "Come What May, I Will Always Love You." His is a beautiful voice, but halfway through, as he looked at his three grown children staring back at him, he choked. Another aunt, his closest sister and confidante, quickly grabbed his mike, put her hand on his shoulder, and finished the song. Meanwhile, my uncle's tears were flowing outward, finally, in front of his entire clan.

That afternoon I watched and listened in amazement as my relatives laid bare their hearts before me. It was as if in poetry we could finally converse about what in prose, in conversation, we couldn't. Words when sung or turned poetic become somehow acceptable and even welcomed in our uncommunicative culture.

As I witnessed their sadness, memories of moments with my own immediate family rushed up before me.

I saw again how timidly my father tried to hold my mother's hand in front of us one evening, and how she, embarrassed, pulled her hand from his grasp and failed to see the subsequent hurt look on his face. In the fifty-odd years that they've been married, my parents, to my knowledge, have hugged twice in public and held hands on one or two rare occasions while they watched TV or strolled the streets near their home in Milpitas, California, after dinner. This practiced repression is as old as the history of Vietnam. "If you love, show the cane" is an age-old adage about how one should raise one's children.

I saw, too, my long-dead paternal grandmother late one night tiptoeing into the living room to put an envelope between the pages of my older brother's math book while we were still new-comers living in a crowded apartment on Mission Street, in Daly City. He had been trying to save enough money to buy a used car so he could drive to college. On the envelope in which she put half of her Social Security income, she wrote succinctly: *"Noi cho con"* (for my grandson).

And I saw myself stuttering that evening long ago, a few years after college, unable to form Vietnamese words when my mother asked, "What's wrong?" Everything was wrong, I had wanted to tell her. The love of my life had left, and I was bleeding inside. But that was not our way, and my Vietnamese is unruly, refusing to give lyrics to the murmurs and pangs of the heart. All I man-aged to say was, "Nothing, Mom, I'm just tired."

I recalled too that first time that I won a journalism award and my father tried, then failed to say something in Vietnamese. Finally, he said it in English: "I'm proud of you," then a quick pat on my shoulder. I was stunned. "Thanks, Dad," I said and looked over to my older brother, whose face was an expression of aston-ishment. He'd said it to the wrong son, and inwardly I was thank-ing myself for refusing to let fulfilling my father's expectations, or failing them, be my goal and foibles in life.

If emotional restraint and proper displays of outward behavior are still considered the utmost beauty in some Confucian mind-sets, and muted endurance is still considered a virtue, these ide-als, when practiced blindly, fail many of us who now live in the complex, modern world called the West. "Show, don't tell" is our millennia-old ethos. But despite my mother's subtle way of saying "I love you" in the impeccable sweet-and-sour catfish soup she serves whenever I visit, the lack of verbal communication leaves me wanting.

And was it not why my lover left me? *Don't leave. I love you.*

A radio commentator and a writer, I am a traitor now to the old ways, for my medium is the written word, and my playground is the public forum onto which my private passions spill. The written words are my songs.

Yet if I manage to say so much in public—and still there is much to be said—I too have failed to say the things I wanted to say to the people I love the most, things that need saying. The old ways, in familial settings, remain overpowering and the tongue refuses to bend, so that the words prepared in reveries are never, by me, spoken.

So—what song did I sing at my uncle's birthday party? I sang many. Songs about broken hearts, about lost innocence. But the one I dedicated to my entire clan was Carole King's "You've Got a Friend." You know the lyrics: "When you're down and troubled and you need some loving care, and nothing, nothing is going right, close your eyes and think of me, and soon I will be there."

It's corny, I know. But it's the only tune I know how to carry well and whose lyrics I have memorized. And it approximated the sentiment I felt. So in front of my family I, too, sang my heart out.

CALIFORNIA CUISINE OF THE WORLD

My sister and I were strolling down Larkin Street in San Francisco one breezy summer afternoon when there wafted by this pungent-salty aroma from some open window above. I was about to name the dish, but the couple walking ahead of us beat me to it. "Hmm, I smell fish sauce," said the blond woman in her mid-twenties. "Yup," her male companion with tattoos on his arms agreed. "Catfish in clay pot. With lots of pepper—and a little burnt."

We had to laugh; he was, well, right on the nose.

Yet when we first came to San Francisco from Vietnam over three decades ago, my paternal grandmother made that dish and our Irish neighbors complained about a "toxic smell." Mortified, we apologized and kept our windows closed whenever Grandma had an urge to prepare some of her favorite recipes.

Many years passed. Though she is no longer around, no doubt Grandma would appreciate the fact that what was once considered unsavory (or even toxic) has become today's classic. For in California, private culture has—like sidewalk stalls in Chinatown selling bok choys, string beans, and bitter melons—a knack of spilling into the public sphere, becoming shared convention.

Or put it this way: the Californian palate has shifted along with the state's demographics, where one in four is now an immigrant. Within a four-block radius from my home, I can have Thai, Chinese, Spanish, Vietnamese, Moroccan, Indian, French, Mexican, Greek, Italian, and Japanese food—not to mention the regular fare at diners and seafood houses.

The theme of hybridity is central to a global society, and a large part of that entails accommodating one's tongue to the delectable world's zests and zings. On its front page in April of 2006, the *San Francisco Chronicle* loudly declared: "America's Mean Cuisine: More Like It Hot—from junk food to ethnic dishes, spicy flavors are the rage." Californians were the first to give up blandness to savor the pungent lemongrass in our soup, and the first to develop a penchant for that tangy burn of spicy chili. It came as no surprise to Californians that Cheez-It came out with "Hot & Spicy" crackers flavored with Tabasco Sauce, that Kettle Foods has "Spicy Thai" flavored potato chips, and that Campbell Soup makes Vietnamese pho beef broth. "There are 15.1 million more Hispanics living in the United States than there were 10 years ago, and 3.2 million more Asians and Pacific Islanders," said the *Chronicle*. "And the foods of those countries—longtime favorites with Californians—are now the nation's most popular."

California wine, famous around the world, with over thirteen hundred operating wineries, dominates the American sense of culinary elegance and accounts for over 90 percent of total U.S. wine production, or the equivalent of 3.12 billion bottles of wine. The pasta bar, San Francisco sourdough bread, the screwdriver and mai tai and margarita cocktails, wine bars, and the steak-and-lobster dinner all originated in the Golden State. For that matter, so did Mandarin and Szechwan cooking, Mexican and Thai food, fortune cookies, French dip sandwiches, cioppino, and so on.

And let's not forget that greatest cooking show ever, *Iron Chef*, which before it became a national sensation on the Food Network and spawned two American versions, was first aired in San Francisco in Japanese with Chinese subtitles. Intended for a select ethnic audience, the show nevertheless garnered a large and diverse following, despite the fact that the majority of viewers understood neither Chinese nor Japanese. But crossover is a phenomenon that occurs frequently in California, like earthquakes, and the languages of cooking and competition combined make for an explosive and enthralling conversation. A sake-soaked lobster burning on hot stones with sea kelp, foie gras seared on a burning pan, fresh yellowtail served with daikon radish, and the mad dash to meet the clock—we all watch and salivate and wish to God that we were there as one of the lucky judges.

Well, I was there—sort of. As a well-traveled writer, it turns out that my biggest hit at various dinner parties is not my stories of the time I spent with ex-Khmer Rouge soldiers in Cambodia in the early nineties, nor my trek to the foot of Mount Everest, nor my trip to Kish, Iran, where I talked with long-oppressed Iranian writers, nor my dusty camel ride into the Sahara Desert. No, it's the afternoon I spent interviewing chef Hiroyuki Sakai of *Iron Chef* fame, sipping his Riesling, eating his delicious fried sole, and listening to stories of his wins (the two-hour lobster challenge, his favorite and last show) and losses (hated the live octopus challenge; yelped when octopus wrapped tentacles around his arm). Friends and relatives in California all looked at me in awe when I told this story. It was as if I had come down from Mount Sinai after having dinner with God. "You live like a president," said an uncle-in-law who's a big fan of Sakai.

Irene Khin, chef and owner of Saffron 59, Inc., a catering business for upscale New Yorkers, told me she always regards California as the leading edge: "I have so many friends in California who are into wine and food. And you've got fresh vegetables and large ethnic groups—a great, great combination." Khin, who hails from Burma, consults with many restaurants around the world to come up with suitable fusion dishes. She considers the year-round fresh and "incredibly diverse selection" of vegetables in California a marvelous blessing. In her apartment overlooking Aster Place, Khin said she dreamed of California, especially during wintertime. "I'd love to wake up and go to an outdoor market to see what's available. It's a bit daunting, though, in New York in February." To be on top of the game, to remain what many consider one of New York's top caterers, she said she travels time and again—to California and Southeast Asia—to sample new dishes and get reacquainted with the old.

Globalization is hardly a new concept in California. Latin and Anglo America came to an epic collision here, then gold made the state famous around the globe, and the rest of the world rushed in and created, perhaps for the first time, a global village. Since then layers upon layers of complexity—tastes, architecture, religions, animals, vegetables, fruits, stories, music, languages—have been piling onto the place, making it in many ways postmodern even before the rest of the world struggled to enter the modern era.

Andrea Nguyen, author of *Into the Vietnamese Kitchen: Treasured Foodways, Modern Flavors,* a truly authoritative book on Vietnamese cooking, declared from her Santa Cruz home that "California cuisine is intrinsically ethnic." *El Cocinero Español,* she noted, the first contemporary work on Mexican food in the state, was written a good hundred years ago by Encarnación Pinedo. (Translated into English in 2005 by Dan Strehl, it is now aptly entitled *Encarnación's Kitchen: Recipes from Nineteenth-Century California.*) Nguyen, who remembered her mother packing an orange notebook full of recipes when they were airlifted out of Saigon in 1975, said Vietnamese food is hot these days. "In the Bay Area, you've got restaurants like the Slanted Door, Crustacean, Tamarind, and Bui leading the charge in terms of crossover restaurants."

West has changed the East, indeed, but in profound ways, East too eats West.

It did not always seem so. For the first few years in America my family and I were terribly homesick. At dinnertime, my mother would say, "Guavas back home are ripened this time of year, back at our farm," or someone else would say, "I miss mangosteen so much," and we would shake our heads and sigh. But then a friend, newly arrived in America, gave my mother some seeds and plants. Soon mother's small garden in the backyard was full of lemongrass, Thai basil, Vietnamese coriander, and small red chilies. Homesickness was placated by the fact that home was coming, slowly but surely, nearer to the golden shore.

Now imagine my mother's garden spreading over a large swath of California's farmland. Southeast Asian farmers, in the footsteps of last century's Japanese and South Asian farmers before them, are growing a large variety of vegetables in the Central Valley and trucking them to markets all over the state. Hmong, Filipino, Thai, Cambodian, Vietnamese, Korean, Laotian, South Asian, and Latin American farmers join the rest and sell everything from live chickens and seafood to Thai eggplants and edible amaranth, from hyacinth beans and hairy gourds to oriental squash and winter melons, from Buddha fingers to sugarcane. I, for one, have learned not to underestimate the power of immigrants' nostalgia. In the Golden State, it often becomes retroactive; so much longing for home recreates it in the new landscape. On a sunny day, visiting the local farmers' market, there are fragrances and sounds so oddly familiar that, were I to close my eyes, I could imagine myself back in my hometown, in the verdant, fog-filled plateau of Dalat, Vietnam.

But if California food is intrinsically ethnic, there is another element that is just as essential: the nature of its transgression. It is here that the jalapeño meets star anise and they are paired with a dry, smoky Pinot. Or take the avocado. Though not served in Japanese restaurants in Japan, it is as pertinent to Japanese cuisine in California as sunny skies are to the myth of California living.

And if you haven't tasted a Korean barbecue short-rib taco, popularly known as a kogi, you must. Laced with chili salsa, kimchi and crushed sesame seeds, the kogi is an invention so new that it is sold only from two roaming trucks in Southern California. The drivers post their destinations on the social networking site Twitter, and folks line the streets in Orange County and Los

Angeles—sometimes waiting for up to two hours. Food lovers around the country are waiting anxiously for the trucks to go national. It makes sense that Latin America should meet East Asia in Los Angeles, land of silver screen and American imagination, in one savory bite.

"Foodies are very curious about exotic ingredients," Andrea said. "They're more open to venturing into Asian markets to get the 'authentic' ingredients. They're wanting to explore jujubes, mangosteens, green papaya. Ethnic markets, particular chains like Ranch 99 and Mi Pueblo, are leading the effort to make things easier for everyone. They offer a wide variety of products. And check the aisle carefully—there are often Hispanic ingredients too at Asian markets, like tortillas."

Take the sign that used to hang on the Sun Hop Fat #1 Supermarket on East 12th Street, a few blocks south of Lake Merritt, in Oakland. It said, "American-Mexican-Chinese-Vietnamese-Thailand-Cambodia-Laos-Filipino-Oriental Food." Some saw it as evidence of diversity gone bad, a multicultural mess—that is, too much mixing makes things unpalatable. I, on the other hand, see all those hyphens as complex bridges and crossroads that seek to marry otherwise far-flung ideas, tastes, and styles. After all, creativity is fertile when nourished in the loam of cultural diversity and cultivated with openness and a disposition for experimentation. In terms of food, it results in an explosion of tasty concoctions. Consider some of today's daring experiments: tofu burrito, hummus guacamole, spring rolls with salsa dipping sauce, lamb in tamarind sauce, lemongrass martini, wasabi bloody mary, crab cakes in mango sauce, french fries dipped in mint and cilantro chutney. You see the point: the variety is endless. Today's bold fusion becomes tomorrow's classic.

Seth Bowden, executive chef at Cortez restaurant in San Francisco, known for its creative Mediterranean cuisine with bold flavors (try the baked Monterey squid salad with coco vert beans, and the cod with celery–olive oil mousseline), sums it up this way, "When I think of California cuisine I think of seasonality, Alice Waters, local and extremely fresh ingredients, a freedom from the confines of any one food tradition, and the influence of all the different cultures that make up California's population. And a whole lot of fruits, vegetables, and herbs that are fairly unavailable in the rest of the country. And I think of it pretty much in that order."

I think of it, in some ways, as parallel to my own transnational biography. When the Vietnam War ended I, along with my family (and eventually a couple of million other Vietnamese), betrayed our agrarian ethos and land-bound sentiments by fleeing to California to lead a very different life. Before, my inheritance was simple—the sacred rice fields and rivers that defined who I was. Today, Paris and Hanoi and New York are no longer fantasies but my larger community, places to which I feel a strong sense of connection due to familial relationships and friendships and personal ambitions. Once great, the distances are no longer daunting, but simply a matter of rescheduling. It is not an exaggeration, then, to admit that my tastes have become similarly complicated, taking their reference points from many different continents. Over the years, I've developed a nose for wine and made a habit of pairing it with the various foods that I prepare for friends and family. I've developed a propensity for serving Bordeaux from the Margaux and Haut-Médoc regions, and I've learned to discern the nuances between Oakville Cabernet Sauvignon grapes grown upslope and those grown near bottom.

Indeed, if there's a theme to America 2.0, it is hybridization, remix, and diverse heritages. Ethnic tastes are so in favor that *umami*—Japanese for savoriness—has been proposed as the term for one of the basic tastes sensed by the human tongue. In my lifetime here, I have watched the pressure to move toward some generic, standardized melting-potted center deflate—transpose, in fact—to something quite its opposite, as the demography shifts toward a society in which there's no discernible majority, no clear single center. Instead, the story I often see here is one in which one crosses, to various degrees, from ethnic to cosmopolitan by traversing those various hyphens that hang over the Sun Hop Fat supermarket. When one lives in an age of enormous options in an astoundingly diverse and fertile region where human restlessness and fabulous alchemical commingling are becoming increasingly the norm, one can't help but learn to refine one's taste buds accordingly, to reconcile with the nuances of the world.

How much do food and cooking have to do with my life in California?

I didn't really know the answer until I spent a week at a retreat in Bali recently, fasting and cleansing. For six days straight, I practiced yoga and ate nothing. It was supposed to be a spiritual experience. But it was difficult going, with only a few fruit drinks as my meals.

Hunger, they say, is a good cook. Each night I tossed and turned and became the possessor of strangely vivid dreams. Practically all of them were about cooking and eating. I would sear scallops and fry prawns and toss arugula salads and shave asiago cheese. I would wake each morning slightly disappointed at my failings in this spiritual quest.

But then, near the end of my fast, I had a dream so vivid and real it felt as if I were not dreaming at all: I am back in California, shopping at a local market. I can smell fresh basil. I can touch the glossy red heirloom tomatoes. Then I make this dish that I never made before, a Vietnamese beef stew with a French influence—in which fish sauce and red wine can be mixed and spiced with cinnamon, ginger, and star anise. My good friends gather around a table, waiting for me to serve it. Laughter and cheers ring in the air and there is the clinking of glasses in a shared blessing. I remember thinking, on a very empty stomach: it can't get more divine than that.

IN SEARCH OF HERMES' BELT

Hai called late one evening with the din of Saigon—motorcycle mufflers, horns, laughter—abuzz in the background. "How is everything in 'San Fran'?" he asked.

"Fine," I offered, guardedly.

"I had such fun last time," he said. "Next time, we'll go shopping again."

"Next time," I repeated after him. Having shopped with him, I heard this as a thinly veiled threat.

Let me explain. We met some years ago while I participated in a documentary in Vietnam for PBS. An ad man for a fashion magazine in Saigon, he knew everybody who was somebody in the city. Hai helped set up interviews, introduced me and the film crew to his friends, showed me around my own hometown. So we became friends.

A sweet and friendly man in his thirties, Hai went into the restaurant business with Vietnamese American investors a few years later. Then he became a co-owner of a restaurant chain in Vietnam, and then he decided to visit America—and San Francisco had been in his dreams.

But if I had expected the humble and friendly man I once knew in Vietnam, the one who showed up at my door was someone else entirely—a status-conscious dandy. Empowered by his newfound wealth, he'd become—there's no other way to put it—a brandname whore with three credit cards.

In Vietnam there's a new horde of consumers with dispensable income and a penchant for luxury goods. Small but growing in number, they follow in the footsteps of their Chinese predecessors, traveling the world as shop-till-you-drop tourists. They have Gucci, Shiseido, Nokia, and iPods on their minds. And Hai had become one of them.

Though he spent four days in San Francisco, he did not want to see the Golden Gate Bridge and did not visit Chinatown, nor was he curious about Fisherman's Wharf. Neither the ocean nor the park thrilled him, nor a ride on the cable car. And when I pointed to Russian Hill's shimmering skyline at dusk, he felt obliged to take a picture. Otherwise he was bored. All he wanted to do was shop and eat at the best restaurants and have me take photos of him doing so. The rest of the time he was on the Internet or on his cell phone to talk, yes, what else, shopping.

He had a list of luxury goods he "needed to buy" and since he spoke very little English, I was, besides driver and host and photographer, his interpreter.

I could do nothing but oblige. It was time to pay him back for his generosity when I needed his help back in Vietnam. I dutifully took him around—eating, shopping, and introducing him to my friends, and intermittently recording his American adventures on camera.

Since the Cold War ended, and especially since the U.S. normalized diplomatic relations with its former enemy in 1995, Vietnam's economy had been on a steady rise, growing fast and furious: the GDP average growth had hovered somewhere between 7 to 8 percent annually for nearly a decade. Vietnam may wear the sickle and hammer on her sleeves, but her heart throbs with commerce and capitalism.

It's the age of the Red Bourgeois. And Vietnam is rushing toward consumerist society at a breakneck speed without so much as a backward glance. If religion was once the opiate of the masses, and ideology the cause of revolution, than money has replaced both and converted everyone, young and old, to worship at the brand-new altar of Vietnam called the shopping mall.

In that world, to be able to spend two hundred dollars on a bottle of wine or buy a three-hundred-dollar Gucci shirt is to be the envy of all. It's a world of one-upmanship where, at dinner among friends, the first thing people do is leave their new cell phones on the table to show they've acquired the latest technology. To be rich in Vietnam is indeed glorious. And to be rich requires showing off—lately, by traveling and shopping overseas.

These post-ideological elites—children of business families or high-ranking communists—are now living in a world steeped in wealth and luxury, a world that their parents couldn't possibly imagine a generation or two ago, when they wore black pajamas and stood in line to buy rice from state-owned stores.

This new revolution comes with its own vocabulary:

Di quay: To go wild, to get drunk, to stir up trouble.

Van hoa toc do: Speed culture; culture that moves along at high speed.

Lo Co: Borrowed from "local"—used to describe someone who's backward, a yokel, or to describe cheap goods that are made in Vietnam. None of Hai's friends, he would tell you, is Lo Co. He prefers *Viet Kieu* like me, Vietnamese who return from overseas.

No ("explode"): Slang for someone who spends beyond his or her means in order to show off.

But it's a country of dazzling wealth and humiliating poverty. While the yearly per capita income was $726 in 2006, luxury brands like Shiseido, Prada, Bvlgari, and Hermes were becoming increasingly common consumer goods. A true communist politburo member wouldn't be caught dead these days without a Lexus and a Rolex and at least five servants in his villa. According to a recent survey by the advertising and marketing agency Mindshare Vietnam, 68 percent of youngsters say brand is their biggest concern when buying, and 73 percent are ready to pay more for products with high quality.

And Hai was leading the pack. He was, among other things, obsessed about belts and had a collection by top designers. On his last shopping day, we spent four hours at Hermes. We tested the patience of the young saleswoman who called and searched online all over the country for a blue belt with a big silver buckle in the shape of the letter H—price tag $670—while we sipped our cappuccino.

When she failed to find one, Hai complained in Vietnamese: "I didn't know San Francisco's so limited. They have more choices in Bangkok."

I held my tongue but the young woman asked, so I translated. She apologized. Then, quietly, she asked, "So, are you from Vietnam as well?"

I wanted to tell her that long ago I fled. That when the communists came into Saigon in 1975 and renamed it Ho Chi Minh City, they got rid of the bourgeois class like me and my family and sent many others to re-education camps and new economic zones, our homes confiscated. Others fled out to sea as boat people. Many died.

But if the communists aimed to create a classless society, they failed miserably and the opposite has happened. They found a life of luxury in the abandoned villas irresistible. When the Cold War ended, so began a status-conscious, money-grabbing, hyper-materialistic society the likes of which Vietnam had never seen before in its long, wretched history.

"No," I told the saleswoman, thinking of Joan Didion's book about greed and extravagance. "But it's where I *was* from."

STRESS, VIETNAMESE-STYLE

At an ultra-chic bar called Nam Kha, a well-dressed woman in her mid-twenties named Tram tells me that she's "si-tret." She speaks Vietnamese but switches to English for a word heard often here. There is no equivalent word in her language. The closest you can get is *cang thang than kinh*—tension of the mind.

Stress is probably the biggest trend to hit Vietnam from America since MTV. At first glance it seems impossible: Vietnam, after all, is a country full of hardworking young people, and rural life is backbreaking for the majority. Generation after generation has known nothing but sweat and toil. But stress is a phenomenon not of simple hard work. It is a kind of symptom associated with young, upwardly mobile urban professionals in peacetime.

One is "si-tret," therefore, like Huy Phan, thirty-two, an ad executive for Tien Phong publishing company, an association of lifestyle magazines. This evening at the Nam Kha bar he has lost his voice after talking nonstop for four hours with clients, models, and photographers on his expensive cell phone. "It's always like this," Huy complains. "It's my day off, but I never stop working. I'm terribly si-tret."

Vietnam's upwardly mobile urban young are given to multitasking these days. Next to Huy, Tram is talking on one phone, ordering a drink, conversing with another friend, and yes, text messaging on another cell phone—all at once. "I have a headache almost every night," Tram complains. "I never had this kind of headache until I got my new job." Her new job: overseeing dozens of young saleswomen in a cosmetics company.

Huy and Tram are quick to acknowledge that they are a privileged group with opportunities unavailable to previous generations in communist Vietnam. Just a generation ago more or less everyone had to stand in line to buy rice, and moving from city to city was a prohibitively complex task that required navigating Vietnam's heavy bureaucracy. These days, young twenty- and thirty-somethings like Huy vacation regularly in Thailand and Singapore. Huy has traveled twice to the United States. Tram flies to Thailand every few months to "de-si-tret" herself. How? "I go shopping," she laughs.

The owner of Nam Kha, on the other hand, says he's not si-tret. Duc Phan, thirty-two, one of three partners who own a growing conglomerate of silk stores, restaurants, and resorts in Vietnam, is gentle and calm. He tells me his secret. "I have very good managers," he says, smiling and patting the shoulder of a handsome young man standing next to him. "They si-tret on my behalf."

Vietnam is a heated economy, in Asia second only to China in terms of growth. Tourism, too, is increasing. Bob Bannerman, who works for the U.S. consulate in Ho Chi Minh City, says that he has seen a shift toward more economic and political transparency here in the last few years. "More and more foreigners are coming in to invest," says Bannerman. "Vietnam wants to be taken seriously now, and there are many smart young people doing amazing things here."

But success comes with a price. The newspapers are full of stories of young people who commit crimes of greed. A story that ran recently in *Tuoi Tre*, a youth newspaper, is a case in point. A young man seduced a teenage girl, and when his cell phone business went belly up he murdered her and took all of her expensive belongings in order to pay back his debtors.

Bao Nguyen, twenty-eight, a flight attendant who also owns a cosmetics store, says he must constantly purchase new, expensive toys to fit in with his business circle. "I bought a five-hundred-dollar cell phone, and everyone in my circle has one. So I bought a new one for twelve hundred dollars, and now I'm respected. It's materialistic, but in my business, you have to do it." And yes, he is often si-tret. But "to de-si-tret," Bao says, "I go to spas and get pampered. It's popular now, even among men."

In a 2002 report by the Pew Center, of forty-four countries surveyed, Vietnam was the most optimistic. A whopping 98 percent of Vietnamese said they expect their children to be better off.

"Vietnamese are experiencing stress now because life is no longer routine," says Michael, an American businessman who declined to give his full name and who has lived in Vietnam for three years. "Or rather, new routines must be learned, and learned quickly in a society that's going through enormous transition."

Yet as someone who speaks fluent Vietnamese, I cannot help but detect a hidden bragging tone within the familiar complaints of the upwardly mobile here. When a Vietnamese says he is si-tret, he is also saying, "I'm doing something important, and I'm successful, and this is the price I'm willing to pay for it."

Huy, meanwhile, is buying everyone at the counter a drink. "I just made a big sale. Come on, drink up," he says hoarsely, just as his cell phone starts to ring again.

TOO MUCH SELF-ESTEEM CAN BE BAD FOR YOUR CHILD

In the age of MySpace and YouTube and Google Earth, the space between East and West seems to shrink. But in the area of self-perception, especially, there remains a cultural gap that can often be as wide as the ocean.

Take Jeong-Hyun Lim, a twenty-four-year-old business student in Seoul, popularly known as Funtwo on YouTube. His rock rendition of Pachelbel's Canon has turned him into a global phenomenon. Lim's dizzying sweep-picking—sounding and muting notes at breakneck speed—has had some viewers calling him a second Hendrix. His video has been viewed on YouTube twenty-four million times so far.

But Funtwo himself is self-effacing, a baseball cap covering much of his face. No one knew who he was until Virginia Heffernan wrote about him in the *New York Times* last August. She called his "anti-showmanship" "distinctly Asian," adding that "sometimes an element of flat-out abjection even enters into this act, as though the chief reason to play guitar is to be excoriated by others."

Anyone in the West with this kind of media spotlight and Internet following would hire an agent and make a CD. But Lim told Heffernan, "I am always thinking that I'm not that good a player and must improve more than now." In another interview, he rated his playing around 50 or 60 out of 100.

Lim's modesty is reassuringly Asian, echoing the famous Chinese saying "He who is not satisfied with himself will grow." In a classic 1992 study, psychologists Harold Stevenson and James Stigler compared academic skills of elementary school students in Taiwan, China, Japan, and the United States. It showed a yawning gap in self-perception between East and West. Asian students outperformed their American counterparts, but when they were asked to evaluate their performances, American students evaluated themselves significantly higher than those from Asia. "In other words, they combined a lousy performance with a high sense of self-esteem," notes Nina H. Shokraii Rees, author of *School Choice 2000: What's Happening in the States*, in an essay called "The Self-Esteem Fraud."

Since the eighties, self-esteem for students has been promoted in many school programs, based on the belief that academic achievements come with higher self-confidence. Rees disputes that self-esteem is necessary for academic success. "For all of its current popularity, however, self-esteem theory threatens to deny children the tools they will need in order to experience true success in school and as adults," she writes.

A quarter-century after Stevenson and Stigler's study, a comprehensive new study released last February from San Diego State University maintains that too much self-regard has resulted in college campuses full of narcissists. In 2006, researchers said, two-thirds of the students had above-average scores on the Narcissistic Personality Inventory evaluation, 30 percent more than when the test was first administered in 1982.

Researchers like San Diego State University professor Jean Twenge worried that narcissists "are more likely to have romantic relationships that are short-lived, at risk for infidelity, lack emotional warmth, and to exhibit game-playing, dishonesty, and over-controlling and violent behaviors." The author of *Generation Me: Why Today's Young Americans Are More Confident,*

Assertive, Entitled—and More Miserable Than Ever Before,
Twenge blames the self-esteem movement for the rise of the
"MySpace generation."

Has the emphasis on self-confidence gone too far in America?
Twenge seems to think so. She points to the French tune "Frère
Jacques" sung in preschool, for example. French children may
still sing the equivalent of "Brother Jack! You're sleeping! Ring
the bells!" But in America the once innocuous song has been converted to: "I am special! I am special! Look at me!" No surprise
that the little train that could is exhausted: it's been laden with
super-sized American egos.

That Asian-Americans dominate higher education in the last
few decades in America is also worth noting. Although they make
up less than 5 percent of the country's population, Asian Americans typically make up 10 to 30 percent of the student bodies at
the best colleges. In California, Asians form the majority of the
University of California system. And at the University of California, Berkeley, Asian freshmen have reached the 46 percent
mark. Also worth noting is that, of the Asian population in the
United States, two out of three are immigrants, born on a continent where self-esteem is largely earned through achievements,
self-congratulatory behaviors are discouraged, and more impor-
tantly, humility is still something of a virtue.

In the East, the self is best defined in its relation to others—
person among persons—and most valued and best expressed only
through familial and communal and moral deference. That is far
from the self-love concept of the West—where one is encouraged to look out for oneself, and truth seems to always originate
in a minority of one. And I fear the far end of that experiment
will result in collective apathy.

In much of modernizing Asia, of course, individualism is making inroads. The Confucian culture that once emphasized harmony
and unity at the expense of individual liberty is now in retreat.

But if there's a place in Asia that still vigilantly keeps the ego in check, if not suppressed, it's the classroom, for good and bad. In Asia, corporal punishment is still largely practiced. Self-esteem is barely a concept, let alone encouraged. Critics argue that though not known to foster creativity, an Asian education, with its emphasis on hard work and cooperation, still largely provides the antidote to the culture of permissiveness and disrespect of authority of the West.

In the West, the words "kung fu" largely represent the martial arts. They have a larger meaning in the East: spiritual discipline and the cultivation of the self. A well-kept bonsai is good kung fu. So is a learned mind, and so, for that matter, is the willingness to perfect one's guitar playing. East and West may be commingling and merging in the age of globalization, but beware—that ubiquitous baseball cap that Funtwo is wearing on YouTube can mislead. It houses very different mentalities in Asia—for when it comes to the perception of self, East and West remain apart.

FROM MAO TO YAO MING

A startling moment when China turned a decisive corner: a man carrying two plastic bags, one in each hand, stood directly in the path of a column of armored tanks, effectively preventing them from proceeding down the avenue toward Tiananmen Square in Beijing.

The day before, on June 4, 1989, hundreds of pro-democracy students and workers had been gunned down in and near the square. The image of "Tank Man," as he's now called, stays indelibly in the mind. Some have said the name of the nineteen-year-old student, whereabouts unknown, is Wang Weilin. There is speculation that he either was executed or is living in exile in Taiwan. Whoever he is, wherever he is now, dead or alive, it is certain that for a brief moment he managed to stop the machines with just his body. This unknown rebel, unarmed, stood up against the awesome power of the state and, as the world watched, gained something priceless in return: he liberated his body from the collective, from being subservient to the ideological machine, and opened the floodgates to a next world.

Although direct political confrontation failed, a new sideways rebellion began in the cultural and economic sphere, one that has succeeded. If Mao launched the cultural revolution in 1966 to be rid of "liberal bourgeois" and to continue the revolutionary class struggle, the bourgeois liberals have struck back. The real cultural revolution, stoked by individual desires and ambitions, is happening now. "The level of societal openness and individual freedom now enjoyed by the people in China was unthinkable to the protesters at Tiananmen Square," says Ling-chi Wang, professor emeritus of Asian American studies at UC Berkeley.

It is not ideology or collective yearning that asserts itself in the Middle Kingdom, but the physical self coming to full consciousness. The civilization known for Confucian morals, Taoist mysticism, and martial arts—ways of looking at the self in relationship with the cosmos radically different from those of the West—has wholeheartedly embraced Western culture and mores. "Economic and educational opportunities, readily available telecommunications, and the Internet have made the people of China highly mobile and quite well informed," says Wang, but also "more individual-centered and therefore, less committed to traditional extended family and Confucian social ethics." Ancestral worship, though allowed under communism, is on the wane as many now flock to the temple of the body. The We of the old traditional world of clanship, of self defined by proper behavior and relationships within the collective, is ceding to the Me of the new generation, one defined by sex.

Premarital sex is now widely practiced. In a 2007 poll by Renmin University of China, more than half the Chinese surveyed in ten provinces found premarital sex acceptable. Only 12.8 percent said it was immoral. In a Beijing study conducted by Li Yinhe, a sociologist at the Chinese Academy of Social Sciences, nearly three-quarters of residents polled said they had sexual relations before marriage, compared with just 15.5 percent in 1989, the year of the massacre. And the Internet, to which two hundred million now have access in China (according to *PC World*), has flung open the bedroom door. While the government cracks down on online political dissent, the new socialism allows for a great deal of personal expression.

Women bloggers are becoming famous for discussing their sex lives online. One even taped the sounds of her lovemaking and managed to crash the host server when too many tried to listen at the same time. A huge Internet celebrity sex scandal in 2008 (now called Sexy Photos Gate) featured Edison Chen, a young Hong Kong hip-hop artist and actor. In some thirteen hundred explicit photos, Chen, a heartthrob featured in *People* magazine's 2006 "Sexiest Man Alive" issue, is seen having sex with over a half-dozen Chinese starlets. The more than thirty million page views of the images caused Chinese authorities to wonder about the effectiveness of the firewall.

Along with sexual freedom is the celebration of the self. The proliferation of spas, sports clubs, fashion magazines and shows, beauty products, massages, dance clubs, love hotels, talk shows about sex, underground porn, and obsession with athletes and movie and pop stars all speak to the glorification of the body—in stark contrast to the Cold War era, when having too big a mirror in one's home or even wearing makeup in public could be deemed antirevolutionary. Most telling is the growth of the cosmetic surgery industry. In recent years, more than ten thousand clinics have opened. The number of surgeries for straighter noses, double eyelids, and breast augmentation would suggest that a fair number of Chinese with disposable incomes are rushing for extreme makeovers.

This new self—fit, augmented, overtly sexual, and on display—contrasts dramatically with Chinese body images of the past. "The ancient Confucian tradition was criticized for its contempt for physical activity and respect for the intellect," notes Susan Brownell, author of *Beijing's Games: What the Olympics Mean to China*. "'Those who work with their brains rule, those who work with their brawn are ruled,' a saying from Mencius, has been used for a century to illustrate the traditional Confucian aversion to physical exercise, including sports."

In ancient Rome and Greece, the naked body was sculpted to perfection and generally glorified. During the Renaissance, the human form was rendered not only anatomically correct but profound in refined drawings and paintings. In China, though, the body was kept hidden until the dawn of the twentieth century. To be sure, there were erotic images in ancient China, but they were created during the Taoist-dominated eras as manuals to educate young married couples. Far more typical were the paintings that depict upper-class men and women perched like peg dolls on carved wooden chairs, their hands hidden in the sleeves of beautiful brocades, their faces stoic, inexpressive. To project a cold outward face was to embody moral rectitude.

"The human body in traditional China was not seen as having its own intrinsic physical glory," says China scholar Mark Elvin, author of *Changing Stories in the Chinese World*. Beauty was not dependent on sexual characteristics and attributes, he says, but on artifice and ornamentation—a painted face, silk brocade, the jade bracelet that dangles from the wrist—or alteration, such as the painful and crippling binding of feet.

Contact with the West changed all that. The presence of the pale-skinned, blue-eyed *gwai lo*, "foreign devil," forced a new kind of self-awareness on the East. Take the beautiful cheongsam, a body-hugging dress worn by Chinese women. Developed in cosmopolitan Shanghai around 1900, it originated from its opposite, the qipao—a baggy and loose-fitting dress meant to deemphasize and conceal the wearer's figure that was transformed in the final years of China's last dynasty to reveal curves, waist, bosom, and a lot more skin.

Along with the colonial-era concept of the body as an object of admiration came a more insidious metaphor perpetuated by westerners: the "sick man of East Asia." It was reinforced by caricatures of the frail, opium-addicted Chinese man with a long pigtail. This image of Chinese defenselessness carved a deep wound in the collective psyche. Not surprisingly, the Boxer Uprising, a peasant-based uprising in 1899 to 1901 against foreign influence, had at its heart the belief that the body can achieve invincibility. The rebels were practitioners of martial arts, which they believed could help turn their bodies into armor, impervious to bullets. That the uprising failed and the bullets did pierce their flesh did not extinguish this collective longing for inviolability. The theme of Chinese martial arts as the antidote to Western conquerors' firepower continues to inform and inspire many films, novels, and comic books.

Under Mao, the body was once more inducted to represent the nation. In propaganda posters that have become collectors' items, workers are depicted as strong and square-jawed; athletes are lithe and agile. Sports became synonymous with modernity. A strong body reflected national strength and was seen as necessary for unity. The self was in service to a larger cause, and everyone moved together wearing Mao jackets—a sea of blue and gray. The body, subdued by ideology, was not yet free.

Freedom arrived in the late 1980s, and its symbol was that singular image of Tank Man engaging in a brazen and courageous act of self-expression. Once unleashed, though, freedom created a ripple effect (more like a wave) that surged through the culture and threatened to wash away hundreds of years of social mores—the piety of Confucianism, the humiliation of Western imperialism, the righteousness of communism under Mao, all variants of a single unifying characteristic: shame.

"Lead the people with excellence and put them in their place through roles and ritual practices, and in addition to developing a sense of shame, they will order themselves harmoniously," Confucius said in his *Analects*. Shame, in other words, binds the tongue and inhibits behavior. Those who seek to change the old world order, on the other hand, learn to be shameless. Lewis Hyde, in his book *Trickster Makes This World: Mischief, Myth, and Art*, noted that artists who seek to change the conversation of the culture refuse "their elders' sense of where speech and silence belong, they do not so much erase the categories as redraw the lines."

Ang Lee's movie *Lust, Caution* is a good example of this realignment. In it Tony Leung, as a merciless Japanese informant in World War II Shanghai, begins his relationship with Tang Wei, a nationalist, by whipping and raping her. She, in turn, uses her body to get at him. Theirs is a carnal dance toward the gates of hell. Sex is as much the story's forward arc as the movie's assassination plot.

Some movie critics have cattily renamed the movie *Caution: Lust!* But that is the warning that Ang Lee's movie propounds. Both insider and outsider, an émigré from Taiwan to the United States, Lee has a vision that encompasses the Far East and the Wild West, the sacred and profane. He reimagines the past with his movies; he shows copulating bodies to the masses and at the same time warns them against unchecked passions. On top of it all, he spurs the conversation in China about obscenity and about what is and isn't proper behavior.

Consider, too, the controversial body art showcased in Shanghai in 2005, in which traditional brush paintings were drawn on naked models. Images of mountains and rivers, of peonies and songbirds, suddenly migrated from the familiar old paper or silk onto moving forms made of human skin. Most compelling was the female model who had a blue cheongsam with white crested wave motif painted on her body. She was both beautifully clothed and astonishingly naked—and a literal transfiguration of the past.

Indeed, that old sea of blue and gray Mao jackets has been rapidly transformed into a field of a hundred thousand flowers blooming, and China's great leap forward is now.

In the age of globalization, the more rigid the politics, the more mellifluously culture can serve as counterpoint, forcing change. Protesters in Tiananmen Square may have failed in their direct confrontation with the state, but in their wake rises a culture all at once playful, shameless, and disruptive of the past—and the effect is that the nation, unclothed at last, is losing, slowly but surely, not only its inhibition but also its tongue.

TRAGEDY AND THE
NEW AMERICAN CHILDHOOD

Let me tell you a story. Once upon a time in a village full of ninjas there lived an orphan named Naruto. Because the head of the village sealed the powerful and malevolent spirit of a nine-tailed fox inside his belly when he was born, whenever Naruto lost control of his emotions, the fox took over and caused great havoc.

Naruto knew tragedy intimately. His own parents were killed in a war; Sasuke, his best friend, lost his entire clan to a murderous brother and became hell-bent on revenge; Jiraya, Naruto's favorite teacher, was murdered by another student, named Pain, whose aim was to destroy the world. The newest member to join Naruto's ninja team, Sai, in order to graduate from his martial arts school, had to kill many of his classmates.

Magic, romance, and martial arts aside, the story of Naruto is arguably on par with horror master Stephen King's novels. Except Naruto is a wildly popular Japanese manga (comic book or graphic novel) and anime (Japanese animation) series seen all over the world, including the U.S. Despite the subject matter, it falls into what we used to understand as children's entertainment.

Manga and anime have been a global phenomenon for two decades or so, and their popularity reached its peak at the turn of the millennium. Yet while many articles have been written about the ebb and flow of Eastern and Western cultural influences in the age of globalization, and in particular the enchantment of the West by Japanese pop culture, what is barely touched upon is how the modern-day American childhood is increasingly informed by a set of narratives that diverge radically from those told to children a generation or two ago.

To put it simply: on TV and on the Internet and in graphic novels, Naruto and company are staggering in the footsteps of Job. There are few soft landings, very little candy-coated protection in these story lines from the Far East. For behind those round, puppy- eyed, and cuddly characters with their perfect Western features is a set of ancient Eastern sensibilities informed by human sufferings rarely encountered before in the land of happily ever after. It is why I, now in middle age, as someone who once fled a wartorn country, watch Naruto religiously.

A few years ago in Tokyo, I asked professor Koike Kazuo, the celebrated author of the Lone Wolf and Cub manga series and many others, about the difference between Japanese and American comic books and he said, "Japanese mangas tend to deal with complex characters that are suited for both children and adults." Superman, Green Lantern, and other superheroes, he said, "are too overwhelming, like the U.S. military forces with their high-tech weapons. You grow up and get bored by them." Not so with Japanese protagonists. "The characters may have some powers, but they are vulnerable. They might be beaten by somebody, and people who read manga sympathize deeply with these characters."

Since manga can deal with modern demands, depicting family relations and love, he said, good mangas have plenty of adult readers in Japan, and many are treated on the same level as contemporary novels. "If Superman and Spiderman have wives and kids and real domestic dramas," Koike said, laughing, "they will have adult readers."

Koike, a history professor, could speak with authority. The first issue of the Lone Wolf and Cub series U.S. edition sold around 120,000 copies in the late seventies, making it the best-selling manga in the United States for decades. The epic became one of the longest TV shows in Japanese history, and a six-film series. It's the story of a samurai who takes his baby boy, Daigoro, on the "road to hell" and becomes an assassin for hire while seeking vengeance against Retsudo, the powerful man who ordered the massacre of his clan and framed him for plotting to murder the shogun. Daigoro grows up watching his samurai-turned-assassin father slash, stab, and chop their enemies. In the final confrontation, with his father slain and Retsudo, their neme-sis, wounded, the little boy picks up his enemy's spear and rushes fearlessly toward him. Recognizing spiritual kinship in Daigoro's bushido—warrior spirit—Retsudo embraces the boy and, pierced by his own spear, cries out: "Grandson of my heart!"

Not exactly kid stuff in the late seventies, but the other day as I watched two boys around eight or nine reading Koike's manga at a local bookstore, where half a dozen or so children and teenagers sat on the ground, their backs against bookcases and walls, with graphic novels in their hands, all entranced, it would seem that it is, now. And it would also seem that, as a result, the saccharine, happily-ever-after ending as spoon-fed by the church of Disney since the end of World War II is on the wane, or at least seriously challenged. And favored are dark and tragic narratives from the Far East with kinship to some of those folktales once told by the Brothers Grimm and Hans Christian Anderson.

Coined in 1815 by woodblock artist Hokusai, "manga" described his illustrated doodles, or "involuntary sketches or unintentional pictures." But manga didn't turn into entertainment for children in Japan until 1952, nearly a century and a half later, when Tezuka Osamu invented the story of Astro Boy, a robot with a human soul—a modern-day Pinocchio, as it were, but with a lot of firepower—who continues to have many incarna-tions, including a recent American movie.

Since Astro Boy, practically all the sadness, fear, joy, humor, and desire, not to mention aesthetic expressions and various sexual appetites of the Japanese people—a people who still have direct memories of a nuclear holocaust, who have experienced tsunamis and earthquakes—have found expression through graphic narratives. And, in time, they have found audiences throughout the world.

In the U.S., major outlets like Barnes and Noble and Amazon peddle an array of Japanese anime DVDs and mangas and related merchandise. On the various cable TV programs a viewer can watch some dozen anime shows catered to all ages. Most likely, however, one will pick from the thousands of stories—from robot romance to cooking obsession, from teenage alienation to various sexual dramas (including taboo subjects like brother-sister relationships and high school boys falling in love with one another), from government corruption investigations to inter-galactic noir detective series—available online anytime via You-Tube and Vimeo and AniLinkz and an array of other websites at the click of a mouse.

The business—manga, animated films, TV series, and licensed products like dolls and action figures and related video games—has saturated, peaking at around $5 billion by 2005, and has suffered a downhill trajectory ever since. The main cause is, ironically, the enthusiasm of fans worldwide. An army of devoted admirers' constant scanlation—unauthorized scanning, uploading, and translating—is causing the global manga archive to grow online at breakneck speed, readily available for free.

On the subject of anime, Roland Kelts, an American writer with Japanese ancestry, notes in *Japanamerica* that it is "producing quality content at a time when quality is becoming endangered by advances in technology, which are outpacing attempts to control and even monitor distribution. And anime greets the American viewer with an enormous back catalog."

What makes anime a powerful force in the digital age, he observed, "is its quality contents will arguably become even more greatly prized, as discriminating audiences have access to nearly everything and want only what is good."

American animations, like those produced by Pixar and Disney, Kelts notes, are "like bursts of genius," but for a reader wanting to sink deeper and deeper into a fantasy world, there's nothing like the seemingly endless labyrinth of manga and anime, in which there's always something more to discover. Its seduction is long lasting, often into adulthood and on to the grave.

Professor Koike, for his part, found it interesting that the Japanese imagination is what now sells overseas. "I never wrote my stories thinking they would be read by non-Japanese. But I am glad that the world is now fascinated with what we created to entertain ourselves." Then he said, with utmost seriousness, "On the deepest level, serious mangas are about spiritual drama and love."

Indeed, it is the spiritual drama in many of these stories that most interests me. Spiritual drama always moved beneath the unhappily ending folklore and fairy tales I knew intimately, growing up in Vietnam during the war. Those unbearably hot humid afternoons in Saigon, my older siblings and I would often throw a mat on the tile floor in our maternal grandma's room, the coolest in the house, and beg her for a story before siesta. Decades and a continent away, I can still hear Grandma's story-telling voice, low and sad, lulling her grandchildren toward phantasmagorical and melancholic dreams.

In Grandma's stories, noble deeds are rarely rewarded happily ever after, broken love is the norm, and those who do good can be, and often are, punished.

The husband fled after he realized that he had married his long lost sister by mistake, but the faithful young wife kept waiting with their child, and then one night both mother and child turned into stone on the sea cliff...The lovesick princess died and her heart turned into a ruby, and the grieving king had it carved into a teacup—and whenever he poured tea into it, the image of her paramour, the singing fisherman on his boat, appeared and floated to and fro...So that his jealous older brother would live happily with his new bride, the younger brother left home to die in the forest, and overnight he turned into limestone...

Though heartbreaking, these stories carry a mature wisdom in their resolutions.

The loyal wife's virtues were preserved forever in stone, and in time she became a local goddess known as the Stone Waiting for Husband...When the fisherman saw his own image in the ruby teacup he cried and his tears fell into the cup, which melted back into blood and disappeared, and the princess's love was requited at last...The older brother, wracked with guilt for distrusting his only sibling, sat on the limestone and he too died, turning into an areca tree. His new bride followed and she turned into a betel vine. "When you combine the betel leaf and areca nut and a bit of limestone paste and chew, you get a tingling sensation on your tongue," Grandma said as she chewed, then spat red juice into her spittoon, then laughed. "See, your spit turns the color of blood. It's true love, which is always sad and complicated."

Grandmother told fatalistic tales that are thousands of years old, some older than nations, and if they are sad and strange, there is a sound reason for this vein of morbid magic existentialism. Considering how many generations have seen war and experienced natural disasters, and how calamities have a way of destroying hope, these stories are concerned with the spiritual growth of the young, and not with convincing them that they live in a benevolent universe. The old tales have evolved over the millennia as a way to prepare and warn the next generation for cataclysm and grief. And at their best, they serve as medicine for the soul.

It is spiritual drama, therefore, that draws me to *Naruto*. I recognize the Old World's sensibilities in his story and in many others told through Japanese graphic narratives. The nine-tailed fox is, after all, a creature of myth in the Far East as old as the Hydra or the Minotaur in ancient Greek mythology. In China the fox sometimes takes the form of a beautiful woman who seduces kings, and they in turn destroy their own kingdoms.

And despite the age of digital and high-tech wizardry, despite new creative inventions, manga and anime haven't changed much in their core messages, which continue to distill the ancient ethos from a cultural matrix shared between Japan and the rest of East Asia. They say sacrifice for others is more important than individual happiness, that to grow in strength and wisdom one must find something more precious to protect and love than oneself, that there is an inherent beauty in sadness, a spiritual growth to be had from suffering, and that honor and loyalty and duty sometimes far outweigh, alas, romantic love.

Now, as American children mourn Naruto's teacher's murder, as they watch him struggle to retain his sunny outlook so as not to turn, literally, into a destructive monster, it seems the Far East is not so far from the easternizing West.

A year after the Twin Towers of the World Trade Center in New York City were destroyed by terrorist attacks, I went and visited Ground Zero. There were many visitors and gawkers about, and next to me were a few teenagers, with their charming Midwest accents, snapping photos. And as they surveyed the terrible destruction before them—shattered concrete and melted steel of what was once an ivory citadel—one of them said with reverence in his voice, "Man, this is, like, right out of *Akira*!" *Akira*, if you have not read it yet, is a celebrated manga turned anime about a futuristic Neo-Tokyo (rebuilt after nuclear holocaust) in which many children possess psychic powers. After much fighting between them and various political groups, the city is once more destroyed by an explosion that leaves few survivors.

In a post-9/11 world in which waging preemptive wars in the name of peace has become the norm and the sky is full of war drones, and as the polar icecaps melt and the sea keeps rising and polar bears drown, and as the ominous storms keep gathering and growing stronger—if not at our shores then at the edge of our collective unconsciousness—it may very well be that happily-ever-after narratives are no longer the right medicine, and that the stories American children are gravitating toward are alternative fairy tales that can assist them as they bear witness to the churning tides.

OUR MAN OBAMA:
THE POST-IMPERIAL PRESIDENCY

Having come from a country whose wretched history is largely defined by being colonized or fought over by the various empires, and being a reader of the modern novel, I see the rise of Barack Obama as the beginning of the end of a five-hundred-year-old colonial curse.

Decades ago, English still unruly on my tongue, I read a spin-off of Daniel Defoe's *Robinson Crusoe*, but not the way most of my American peers did. I, on one level or another, saw myself in Friday, Crusoe's servant.

A British sailor participating in the slave trade, Crusoe was shipwrecked off the coast of Venezuela. He was alone for some years but managed with his guns to rescue a native prisoner who was about to be eaten by his captors. He named him Man Friday, taught him English, and converted him to Christianity. He taught Friday to call him "master."

James Joyce once noted that Defoe's sailor is the symbol of the imperial conquest, that "he is the true prototype of the British colonist.... The whole Anglo-Saxon spirit is in Crusoe: the manly independence, the unconscious cruelty, the persistence, the slow yet efficient intelligence, the sexual apathy, the calculating taciturnity."

Likewise, all of those who have been colonized and oppressed in the age of European expansionism are embodied in Friday.

Indentured and "saved" by Crusoe, Friday has become, over the centuries, a political symbol of racial injustice, of victims of colonization and imperialist expansion, of slavery. Friday was African, Native American, Asian, Latin American. And Friday was all the children born from miscegenation.

When he was christened, when he called Crusoe "master," Friday essentially lost his autonomy and his past. When he was taught a new language, Friday lost his bearings and the articulation and enchantment of his old tongue.

In the aftermath of the age of European conquest, many went in search of identity—cultural, national, personal—but the legacy remained largely that of an inferiority complex, a kind of grievance trap that was, for those previously subordinated by the West, nearly impossible to escape.

The power structure is stacked against them. Along with that sense of inferiority, their legacy is often disorganization and distrust. Even if no longer conquered, they remain vanquished—in a world redefined largely by the victors; their sense of value is fragmented, their sense of self unmoored. English is the global language of choice. From Western-style clothing to commerce to political dominance, history seems largely defined by the West. Species long known to natives are constantly "discovered" and given Latin and Greek names. Tall mountains are to be "summited" by wealthy westerners while the bent-backed sherpas simply climb. Ancient settlements are destroyed, old temples are razed and the new structures built upon them are christened with the names of Catholic saints. Even the cosmos is crowded with Greek and Roman gods.

For a while, I grieved. Then I resigned myself to the idea that I was fated to live at the empire's outer edge, in a world in which Friday's children were destined to play subservient roles and act as sidekicks. I knew this because I saw it on TV nightly. Friday became Tonto, Mammy, Pocahontas, and Kato. I saw, too, the complexity of my own Vietnamese past ignored or, worse yet, simplified and reduced to faceless figures in black pajamas and conical hats, to serve as props or to be gunned down by American GIs, the wielders of history.

Defoe's narrative has become so deeply institutionalized that it continues to serve as the core premise of Western culture. Growing up as an outsider, the story I internalized was the supremacy of Crusoe's children. It wasn't a conscious narrative, perhaps, but it became in time a cynicism, and a given: no matter how well you perform and how smart you are, you are not to be in the center, in the place of real power.

Until a decade or so ago, when minorities began to play central roles in the movies, the theme of Crusoe's glory continued to play out unimpeded. *The Swiss Family Robinson* as well as *Robinson Crusoe on Mars* and dozens more movies were direct spin-offs, but the book's mythos also provided the backbone for TV shows like *Star Trek*, on which the captain is white and his crew are ethnic and aliens, and contemporary films like *Men in Black*, *Jerry Maguire*, *Pulp Fiction*, and *Lethal Weapon*, just to name very few. In them the ethnic sidekicks help make the main character who he is, reinforcing his character and centrality. With few exceptions, the white man leads, the minority character follows—for such is the shape of the culture and the unwritten rule taught subliminally not so long ago, a curse of superior-inferior fiction that many ingested as fact.

Who knows, then, when the story began to shift?

Perhaps the resistant narratives were there all along, existing as scars on the slave's back, and in pockets in the various regions and with various subjugated peoples waiting to form a chorus, waiting for the right conductor to come along to form a new symphony.

It may very well have begun when the first slave, robbed of his freedom, his language, but not his music, sang his holy howls in the vast expanse of cotton fields, and in time it turned into the blues and gave birth to American music. In literature, it most gloriously began with Frederick Douglass. Lewis Hyde, in his seminal work *Trickster Makes This World,* regards Douglass as a kind of trickster—like Hermes or Loki or Eshu—who learned to reallocate power, a "cunning go-between...[a] thief of reapportionment who quit the periphery and moved to the center."

Born a slave in Maryland in 1818 to white father and black mother, Douglass learned the alphabet from his master's wife. He stole books. He learned how to read and write. He taught others. He became an abolitionist, editor, suffragist, author, and the first African American nominated in the U.S. for vice president, in 1872 on the Equal Rights Party ticket with Victoria Woodhull, the first woman to run for president.

But what did Douglass steal, exactly? The language of the masters, of course; their eloquence. And he mastered it. He spoke up. He thereby crossed the color lines, the demarcations that he was not supposed to cross. He wrote autobiographies: *Narrative of the Life of Frederick Douglass, an American Slave; My Bondage and My Freedom;* and *The Life and Times of Frederick Douglass*—and, according to Hyde, his stories challenged and broke "the rule of silence" and "contest the white world's fiction about slavery," liberating him and, in turn, others.

For this is the way the power lies: those who once dwelled at the margins of the commonwealth have appropriated the language of their colonial masters and they use it with a great degree of articulation as they inch toward the center, crossing all kinds of demarcations, dispelling the old myth. If Crusoe contends that he still is the lead actor, Friday is not content to play subservient and sidekick any longer.

That old superior-inferior fiction is further eroded by the way history flows. The America that received my family and me in the mid-seventies, for instance, was an America that could not possibly fathom the coming of a Pacific Century. The rise of the Far East, its cultural and economic influences lapping now at the American shores, seem to have taken everyone by surprise. Like sidewalk stalls hawking bitter melons and bok choy and lemongrass on the streets here in San Francisco, private passions, too, are spilling out with candor onto the public place. Indian writers—Rushdie, Arundhati Roy, Kiran Desai, Aravind Adiga—have become winners of one of the most prestigious literary awards in the English language, the Booker Prize. Japanese manga and anime—with their particular Japanese sensibilities and angst—have become the prominent genre of children's entertainment. Sushi is being sold in high school cafeterias, HMOs are now offering acupuncture, and feng shui and yoga have become household words.

All the while, unprecedented mass movements from south to north have irrevocably changed the north: salsa vies with ketchup as the top sauce; tango, Latin jazz, Jamaican reggae, and Mexican hip-hop liven up American dance floors; Spanish becomes increasingly the second language of choice; and so on.

If those in America still think of globalization as a one-way trip, that it is simply the Americanization of the rest, they should seriously think again. Even if the spelling checker of my Microsoft Word program refuses them as real words, the Easternization and Latinization of America are changing America as I type.

Obama's rise to the highest office of the land has opened the door wider to that growing public space in which Americans with mixed backgrounds and complicated biographies—Latino Muslims, black Buddhists, gay Korean Jews, mixed-race children—can celebrate and embrace their multiple narratives with audacity. He gives us license to embrace our various inheritances and to reimagine ourselves in an America in which we are equal and at the center.

This too is America: the Hmong girl in Oakland is texting to her Mexican boyfriend in San Jose, who is on Skype with his *abuela* in Oaxaca. The teenager who calls herself Japorican—part Japanese and part Puerto Rican—and the boy who is Chirish—part Chinese, part Irish—are pushing the stroller carrying their global-village baby toward some intricate future.

No, I am not so naive as to believe we have moved into a Utopia. Fear of the other will continue, of course, and bigotry and racism, and fighting over resources and for power. Many who believed in democracy and fair play when they were at the center find those ideas troubling when Friday's relationship with Crusoe suddenly and radically changes. Yet I cannot help but be optimistic, for is this not the original promise of America: "E pluribus unum"—out of many, one?

And if the Vietnamese teenage refugee was once overwhelmed by his losses, his inferiority complex, and by his alienation on the Western shore, the Vietnamese American writer, through his struggle to find words to redefine himself, has become a bona fide cosmopolitan. The world I live in now, indeed, requires communicating across time zones and hemispheres, traveling from one continent to another, and negotiating among different languages, dissimilar cultures, and once far-flung civilizations.

———

It was Defoe's conceit in his novel—published in 1719 and considered by many to be the first novel written in English—that the "savage" could only be redeemed by assimilation into Crusoe's culture and religion. It was beyond Defoe's power of imagination to see how much Friday, in time, could radically change Crusoe, and that the world of Crusoe was forever altered by having absorbed Friday.

On that fateful Tuesday, November 4, 2008, Friday spoke up loud and clear and declared himself an equal, and his voice is heard around the world. He has become the conductor of a new movement. He tells us all to dare dream big, and to reimagine ourselves and therefore reimagine America itself.

The old curse ends. Some internalized threshold for previously subjugated people is breached. To live in America fully these days is to learn to see the world with its many dimensions simultaneously. And where others hear a cacophony, the resident of the cosmopolitan frontier discerns a new symphony. His talent is the ability to overcome the paralysis induced by multiple conflicting narratives and selves by finding and inventing new connections between them. He refutes simplification and holds opposed ideas in his head without going crazy. He knows now it's within his powers to articulate and reshape his new world and, regardless of the color of his skin, play a central character in the script of his own making.

PH(O)NETICS

Pho, that ingenious Vietnamese concoction, is an incomparable and sacred broth. Spiced with roasted star anise, cardamom, cloves, cinnamon, charred ginger, and onion, and made savory by fish sauce, the soup is brewed at a low heat until the beef falls off the bone and the marrow seeps. It inspires passion, and it is as endemic to Vietnamese culture as the Vietnamese language itself.

But since the Vietnam War ended, the soup, too, has become like the Vietnamese diaspora—a global, well, phonomenon.

So much so that among my own clan, whenever we gather from all over the U.S., Canada, France, and England—to celebrate a wedding, say, or mourn the passing of a relative—"pho-talk" often tops the list of our conversational topics. "I was in Athens last year and guess what?" Someone will start, and someone else will rise to the challenge. And so begin the rowdy banter and tall tales.

It is a kind of game of one-upmanship, both to show off our new cultivated selves and to marvel at how far we've come since our initial expulsion from our beloved homeland. For within the culinary experience is the theme of our journey itself. Cousin B, the rowdy kid back home, has become a manager for a big high-tech company and travels widely. He has eaten pho in Rio de Janeiro. Uncle P., who lives in France, has eaten pho in Tanzania.

Friends and relatives have eaten pho in Hong Kong, Tokyo, Jakarta, Mexico City, Paris, London, Melbourne, Seoul, Bangkok, and yes, even far-flung Dubai and Johannesburg. We gossip. We tell pho stories, often while savoring the soup. It's as if knowing another far-flung city that serves what was once our national treasure eases our nostalgia and appeals to our hope for prosperity: wherever there's Vietnamese, there's pho.

...*In Ubud, Bali, Vietnamese pho has taken on a delicate taste. Served with fresh snow peas and a wedge of lime and no other garnish to speak off, except a sprig of an amazingly spicy and fragrant basil, it's a delight, especially when the waitress blesses the soup with a white orchid to enhance the spirit of the broth.*

...*I happened to be in this outskirt area of Sydney and read about a museum that was putting up an "I (heart) Pho" exhibition, right. It took me a second to realize that it was an exhibition of our soup. So I went, of course. They served pho inside the museum and even imported a pho stall from Saigon, to reconstruct Saigon street food inside the museum. Then I saw teacher P. from Le Qui Don high school. Can you believe it? Of course, we ate pho together. So far from Saigon, but there we were, teacher and student, three decades later, sitting on a wooden bench, slurping, laughing, just like old times—except we were on another continent.*

...*In Nargakot, Nepal, high above the clouds, there's this hotel that sometimes serves pho on weekends. Beef is not available but buffalo meat is used. The meat is a little bit chewy. But with such clear air and strong wind, everyone—the tourists, the people in town— everyone knows when they're making pho, even the bloody yetis.*

...*Okay. I was craving pho so badly after a year working in Namibia. There's no Vietnamese around to speak of, except—I know, I know, God strike me down for what I'm about to say—the Vietnamese commies' embassy. One day I walked by and the smell of pho wafted out. Mind you, I hate them commies. They sent my father to the re-education camp and I was a boat person myself. But I couldn't help it. I salivated like a dog and found myself ringing their bell. Asked if I could buy a bowl of pho from them. This is how pathetic I was. And this guy, real young, thirties at the most, laughed and said,*

"*Brother, why don't you come in and eat with us?*" *I hesitated for a second. And went in. I'm not proud of it. But some things transcend politics.*

...Did you read about "the story of Fo"? So this Vietnamese man who joined the merchant marine when the war ended, he was homesick of course, but there's no home to go back to. So he kept on sailing. One day he ended up on this island called Reunion. Far down the beach, he saw a little makeshift restaurant with coconut trees and thatched roof and, though he should really have been getting back, he headed for it. A dark-skinned, elegant-looking mademoiselle greeted him with a bright smile and gave him the menu. Conch and fish, he'd had plenty, but as he scanned the menu with the boredom of someone who had eaten too many exotic meals, he saw at the bottom of the page a word that caused him to sit up and stare: "Fo."

You guessed it. It's pho but after many generations. Still, who would complain about spelling when the broth simmered in the kitchen? There was no rice noodle to what survived, no star anise smell, not even fish sauce. The mademoiselle with a slender figure and a bright smile made noodle out of tapioca. She rubbed it into uneven strings between her dexterous fingers, then boiled them.

Yet it was "un plat Vietnamien." *Green onion was sprinkled on the soup and a waft of ginger was enough to tell him* "quelque saveur de son pays" *had indeed survived. When he asked her how it was that a Vietnamese-like dish ended here, she shrugged and said,* "Mais, moi aussi, j'suis Vietnamienne"*—I'm also Vietnamese.*

"But how? Impossible!"

"Five generations ago. But I'm still Vietnamese. It was my ancestors who left me the recipe," *she said with utmost seriousness.*

Five generations ago! He searched his high school memories and a piece of history made itself clear through the monotonous voice of a flint-skinned, bespectacled teacher who smoked while he lectured. In 1888, the French exiled King Ham Nghi and his entourage when they refused to follow French rules.

The story ended when he was late for his ship. Incroyable, non?
...Did you hear the story about a pho place in a colony in Antarctica? This Vietnamese woman, right, she's married to a scientist and they lived there and among the tundra and glaciers and penguins she grew bored. So one day...

Have broth, will travel.

Here's mine...

I was young then, barely out of college. While backpacking through Europe, I was invited on an excursion by a friend from UC Berkeley, my alma mater, who knew someone who lived in a castle in Belgium. "It's a surprise," she told me and said nothing more. We got off a train in the middle of nowhere, north of Brussels. And walked for half an hour. We passed pastures and ranches and then we entered a wood. Then, there it was, a castle with its drawbridge across a moat. There were roman statues on the lawn. I remember stopping on the drawbridge and sniffing. I hadn't expected it. But there it was, that complex aroma wafting in the air—cinnamon and cloves and fish sauce and star anise and beef broth. Someone was making pho!

On that summer afternoon, standing over a moat with my friend ahead beckoning me to enter the European castle, that pungent and savory aroma seemed to have wafted across several continents. Smelling it, I had something close to an out-of-body experience. The smell of my Vietnamese childhood had superimposed itself on a new landscape, and all at once I was happy and nostalgic, and I felt that, though I wouldn't admit it to myself for a few years yet, were I to become a writer I would try to capture that delightful sense of transnational dislocation.

I followed my friend down the stone steps to an enormous kitchen, one that could easily fit thirty chefs. At its far end stood an elegant Asian woman in her mid-thirties. She greeted us with a gracious smile and she spoke in Vietnamese. "There you are! I've been waiting and waiting. I thought you got lost in the woods."

As she fed us her pho soup, she told her story. Once a high school teacher in Saigon, she'd lost her job after the war. One night she and her sister fled in a crowded boat out to sea. A Belgian merchant vessel picked everyone up and brought the lot back to Belgium.

Impoverished, she and her sister resorted to living in the basement of a church in a town outside Brussels. One day, a local baron, who had hoped to become a priest but his family forbade it, saw her while he was praying in church. They looked at each other. He fell in love. She was hesitant. But they married. Now the mother of two children of noble blood, she would sometimes catch glimpses of herself as she glided past the gilded mirrors along the old castle's corridors and shudder, wondering, Who is that? Is that me? Other times, when entertaining European royalty, she felt as if she were on a movie set and kept waiting for the director to yell "Cut!"

—— —

These days if you search the Internet for the words "pho soup," you'll likely get tens of thousand of hits, from Wikipedia to various chefs giving recipes and writers waxing enthusiastic to critics providing reviews and scholars writing academic papers on the soup's origins. The Campbell Soup Company took it mainstream in 2002 by canning pho broth and aiming it at mainstream eateries. Even Food Network has chefs teaching its audience how to make pho.

But just where did this soup come from? What's almost certain is that it came from North Vietnam, specifically Hanoi, about a century ago. What is less certain is how. Seminars on the dish have scholars from all over the world arguing whether the word came from the French word *feu* ("fire," as in the dish *pot-au-feu*) or whether it descended from the word *fen*—Chinese for "rice noodle." Star anise, native to southwest China, is used in combination with Vietnamese fish sauce to give pho its distinctive flavor, but French onion is also used, to sweeten the broth. Cardamom comes from India but noodle is definitely Chinese. Yet in Vietnam beef was rarely used until the French came in the late 1800s.

It may sound like a contradiction to say that a distinctly Vietnamese dish most likely has both French and Chinese influences, but it isn't. *Feu* or *fen*, pho is indelibly Vietnamese *because* it incorporates foreign influences. Like the country whose history is one of being conquered by foreign powers and whose people must constantly adapt to survive, the soup has roots in so many heritages yet retains a distinctive Vietnamese taste.

Long ago in parochial Dalat, that lovely hill station the French built on a plateau full of pine trees, I would wake up on the weekend with that exquisite aroma of pho permeating our villa on top of a windblown hill. Downstairs in my mother's kitchen, the clattering sounds of dishes and bowls and chopsticks were welcome music to the ear. I can, despite the years, still hear it: Mother singing downstairs, her ladles clattering against the pots and pans, the steady chopping sounds of the cleaver on the worn wooden block.

That insular, serene world has irrevocably changed and can now only be had in the recalling. So many of us have scattered to all corners of the world. But I take comfort in knowing that that delectable pho aroma, too, has permeated the world.

LETTER TO A YOUNG IRAQI REFUGEE TO AMERICA

Last night on the Internet, I chanced upon an image of you: you—a young teenage boy from Iraq, newly arrived in America—with your shy smile, your bewildered eyes, you remind me of myself a long, long time ago.

Many have stepped onto the American shore since my arrival but few share such parallel tracks as you and I. You and your family fled Iraq; my family and I were once refugees from Vietnam. We both found asylum in a country that had a direct hand in the chaos and bloodshed in our respective homelands. Iraq, it seems, is about to replace Vietnam in the American psyche as the reigning metaphor for tragedy.

I could, as with baseball cards, trade Gulf of Tonkin Incident for Weapons of Mass Destruction, My Lai Massacre for Haditha, boat people for Iraqi refugees, "Hearts and Minds" for "Operation Iraqi Freedom," and "Vietnamization" for "Iraqization." The similarities continue to pile up as the war goes on.

Though I know little of your past, I have an idea of what you're going through. Life in a new country is difficult and bewildering, but for those forced into exile, it torments to the core. You will always grieve for what was stolen from you and your family, and yet, while many perished, or languish still as refugees in Iraq's bordering countries, or face a nightmarish existence back home, you have survived and found your way to the Promised Land.

A new reality is upon you and you must rise to meet it. This entails a drastic change in your nature, in your thinking, and, possibly, in your very constitution.

You will learn soon enough that in the land of plenty there's plenty of irony. The champion of human rights one day can easily become the worst violator of those rights the next. The country that boasts, "Give me your tired, your poor, your huddled masses yearning to breathe free" turns its back on those whose misfortunes are the direct result of its own intervention.

Here, where freedom of expression is written into law, there's very little space to accommodate your biography, your story, and your anguish and distress. For what may be a central concern in one country is often but a footnote in another.

You will find, too, that the American experience in Iraq will, in time, be reconstructed—through books, movies, and songs—into a mythic reality around which the nation flagellates itself and reexamines what now seems its routine loss of innocence. But Iraqis themselves, like the Vietnamese before them, will be relegated to the margin.

The complicated narrative of a civil war with so many sides and so many people caught in the middle will be dismissed until the American experience takes center stage. Everyone else becomes the enemy. That is to say, the faceless, conical-hatted Vietnamese in black pajamas of old Hollywood movies has donned the galabiyya to play the new antagonist in the desert.

But don't give in to the self-indulgence of despair. Do not let bitterness own you, and do not give in to resentment nor be overwhelmed by grief. Despair fuels hatred, and hatred warps you into the very image held by those who think the worst of you. Learn to keep your heart free of hatred and despair.

You have survived, after all, and you must turn your new life into constructive expressions, if not for yourself, then for all those you love, and all that is important to you.

How you do this you must find on your own; you must think it through on your own. I can, from experience, however, tell you this much: you cannot run away from the past, feign amnesia, and embrace the new. I tried this, and it did no good. I learned in time to combat the rancor in my heart by embracing my losses instead. I learned to accept the tragedies of my life: my lost homeland, my murdered friends and relatives, my traumatized family, my broken heart—all my own sadness—as an inheritance. But by "inheritance," I do not mean that the past owns me, but that I learned to appropriate it. Over time, I have learned to give that heritage aesthetic testimony, returning to it again and again, and each time, I find new points of articulation. This gives me solace, a spiritual center, and, ultimately, a sense of direction.

Accept your sadness, then, live with it, let it be part of you as you grow and change, even as you find joy and newness in your adoptive land.

My third piece of advice is this: learn to live with the contradictions of your new home. You must look at this country through two oftentimes opposed lenses: America versus the United States. The two can be as opposed to each other as the olive branch is to the cluster of arrows in the bald eagle's claws on the Great Seal. In good times, America leads and the United States follows. In troubling times, the United States dances alone.

The United States, after all, is a sovereign government with permanent interests, currently waging a war on many fronts. Rhetoric aside, it will trample upon the lives of innocents in its path in order to secure its interests. This it calls "collateral damage," another bitter pill you must learn to swallow.

Yet America remains the ideal that we all aspire to, everything you and I have ever dreamed of—transparency, opportunity, due process, fair play, and a promise of expansion and progress. It is where you work hard and earn respect, build a home and raise your kids, and where, with determination and a clear vision, you can rise to your highest potential. America tolerates difference, understands diversity, and assumes you are innocent before proven guilty. America allows you to practice your religion, protects your privacy, and encourages you to dream. It is a place where you can disagree with your neighbors, your politicians, even your government, without fearing violence or arrest.

While the United States is a fact, even a necessity, America is the deepest promise of this country, fashioned out of the fire of idealism, never fully realized but constantly reimagined and fought over by each generation, a nation *becoming*. Yet accepting the cold reality of what the United States does out of national security interests does not mean you should ever be complacent. You must correct and object to the wrongs, the immoralities and the injustices, that are being waged at home and abroad, for as far as I am concerned, the truest form of patriotism must always be a civilized one.

My fourth piece of advice: in spite of your sadness, ally yourself to this country and let it embrace and transform you as you will undoubtedly steer and transform it.

If you don't believe me, then look at the new faces of America: the Indian writer, the Salvadoran poet, the Chinese actress, the Haitian hip-hop artist, the mixed-race children of many inheritances who are in themselves the fusions of many far-flung ideas. The entire world has entered here and commingled, and the richness of our stories has become, in my humble opinion, America's saving grace. The American experience no longer needs to be monolithic and singular. Instead, a complex, many-voiced chorus is forming. And it needs your voice.

This, then, is my final piece of advice: tell your story. Rage against the impulse to forget. Commit everything: each burnt-out house, each broken body, each wailing mother—all your grief—to memory. Live with your anguish, with your questions, even where there are no easy answers. When you find your voice, sing.

It's your responsibility, your spiritual burden to speak up, to bear, if you can, moral witness to the new tragedy of your generation.

As a Vietnamese refugee who became an American writer, who found his tongue and then his own path in life, I can tell you that you matter, that your sadness matters, that the story of how you survived and triumphed matters.

Even if you don't know it yet, we all desperately need to be reborn through your eyes. For every story that belongs to you, in time, belongs to America.

CAN GHOSTS CROSS THE OCEAN?

When we first came to America a long time ago, Ngoai, my maternal grandmother, suffered a sort of crisis of faith. She prayed and lit incense sticks and tapped the copper gong to call our ancestors' spirits, but she was no longer convinced that her prayers were heard.

What caused Grandma's consternation was the fact that Grandpa, who had died during the Vietnam War, had never once visited her in her dreams in America.

"Child," Grandma would sometimes ask me, "do you think ghosts can cross the ocean?"

"I think so, Grandma," I would answer quickly, if only to make her feel better—but how would I know? All I knew was that back home, Grandma often had dreams in which Grandpa would come and talk with her.

At times it seemed as if they were still a couple living together, those years near the end of the war. When Grandma lost her jade bracelet, for instance, she prayed to Grandpa and he came into her dream and told her where to look. She found it the next day.

Another time Grandma, who had given up writing poetry when she was young, surprised everyone at breakfast by reciting a mellifluous ode to spring and autumn. When we applauded she pointed to the dark rosewood altar and said, "I had help. You should compliment Grandpa as well."

The last time Grandma had seen Grandpa in her dreams was a few months before the end of the war. "You will go on a very

135

long trip and we won't meet for a long time," he predicted. Grandma was perplexed. She couldn't imagine going anywhere but to join him and our ancestors in the spirit world. No one doubted Grandma's dreams. We accepted the presence of ghosts in Vietnam the way we prayed and talked to the dead daily at our ancestral altar. Grandpa's prediction, sadly, came true after communist tanks rolled into Saigon and my family and I had to flee our homeland.

Can ghosts cross the ocean? When I was young, her question struck me as a bit eerie. Now I find it tragic. Once we were bound to the land in which our ancestors were buried and we lived comfortably with ghosts and the idea of death and dying. In America our old way of life quickly faded.

America looks to the future, and not the past; it is moved by the ideas of progress and opportunity. And American people move about, from job to job, from city to city, restlessly. Indeed, where can one's ancestral ghosts dwell in a world of humming computers and concrete freeways and shiny high-rises?

As time passed, Grandma's question came to seem irrelevant for most of her grandchildren—we have gone on to become modern, cosmopolitan Americans, after all. These days, in front of the family altar, with all those faded photos of the dead staring down at me, I often feel oddly removed, as if staring not at the present, but a piece of my distant past. Having fled so far from Vietnam, I can no longer imagine what to say, or to whom I should address my prayers, or for that matter what promises I could possibly make to my dead ancestors, since the most sacred one of all—that I should live and die in my own homeland—has already been broken.

Perhaps I'll never know if ghosts really cross oceans or not, but in one of the last conversations I had with her, when I visited Grandma in her convalescent home, I learned that the question was, for her at least, resolved.

"I was sitting in the garden yesterday," Grandma told me in a happy and excited voice that I hadn't heard for a long time, "and there was this butterfly that kept flying about me. Suddenly, I just blurted out and asked, "Husband, if it is you then come land on my shoulder." And it did, on both sides, and it stayed for a long, long time."

A few days after my visit, Grandma collapsed and fell into a coma. The doctors said there was little chance of recovery. "She could go anytime now," they warned. It was many years before she died.

Yet when I think of my grandmother, it's not a decrepit old body sustained by a respirator and IV units that I see. The vision that I keep safe is admittedly a sentimental one, and the one I did not see: A gentle old lady sits serenely in the rose garden at dusk, smiling happily. A flock of butterflies alights upon her bony frame, their wings forming a golden blanket for her in the last light.

BUDDHA AND ANCESTRAL SPIRITS IN SUBURBIA

I

On a small street in East Palo Alto, a block away from the Bayshore Freeway that connects the high-tech hubs of Silicon Valley, there's a distinctive two-story Vietnamese Buddhist temple with an upward-curved roof, painted in gold whitewash. Standing at the temple's gate you can hear both the sounds of cars zooming at high speed at a distance and the beating of gongs and deep, resonant Buddhist chanting reverberating from inside the temple. In the cool air, the fragrance of cedar incense wafts and wanes.

It's Sunday and the temple grounds are full of worshippers. The scene is reminiscent of the Vietnamese villages of my childhood. A few girls are jumping rope in a cement courtyard while elderly women gossip as they cook in a large, open-door kitchen. On a wooden bench outside the cafeteria, where vegetarian food is served, a young woman and a young man discuss their educational prospects over lunch. Their parents introduced the two after the sermon.

"The temple is more than a place of worship," says Mrs. Luong Nguyen, who insists that I eat the vegetarian food since it's good karma. "We come here to feel anchored. We share news about our lives and we support each other." Then, eying the young couple chatting happily a few feet away, she whispers, her eyes sparkling mischievously, "If possible, we get our children married." On the weekend, along with Buddhism, Vietnamese language is taught to those born in the U.S. whose parents want them to be literate in Vietnamese.

Though it began in 1977, the temple was not built until 1983. Giac Minh temple now serves not just as a place of worship, a monastery, and a gathering place for the community, but also as the headquarters of the Vietnamese Buddhists of America, an organization that includes nearly two hundred Vietnamese Buddhist temples scattered across the United States, five monasteries, and two Institutes for Buddhist Studies serving the spiritual needs of a million Vietnamese Americans. According to its abbot, Thich Thanh Cat, who came to the United States at the end of the Vietnam War and now heads the federation, the temple could have been built in 1979. "But the money we saved for construction all went to sponsoring boat people. That was more important, of course, than having a temple."

A licensed acupuncturist, the abbot poured most of his earnings into refugee aid and temple construction. When enough boat people had settled in the area, they in turn donated their money and labor to finish the temple. Now in his eighties, he devotes full time to "the spiritual needs of my flock."

On any given week, Giac Minh temple hosts a handful of abbots, most of whom received their training here before going on to establish their own temples elsewhere. However, not everyone who joins the monastery becomes a monk, Abbot Thich Thanh Cat tells me. "There are many challenges. We accept anyone who is willing to join, but to stay is another matter."

Abbot Thich Chan Minh, whose temple is in New Orleans, has returned here to give the Qui Y ceremony, the Buddhist version of baptism, to a dozen Vietnamese. All are given new Buddhist names and certificates, and the story of Buddha is retold as they sit on the floor cross-legged with bowed heads. "Buddha is not out here but in each of you," he says, in a clear but gentle voice, "so be kind to one another, be kind to your husband, to your wife, to your children, because when you are cruel to one another, you are cruel to Buddha."

Most of the monks and nuns must support themselves and their temples by working at secular jobs. Abbot Thich Giac Phuoc, for example, a monk in his early thirties, runs a temple in Los Angeles while working full-time as a pharmacist. "It's not an easy task, which is why I come back here for instructions and guidance whenever I can."

Abbott Thich Giac Hoang, an older monk who runs a temple in Washington, D.C., worked for twelve years as an engineer but now devotes full time to the temple. "We all have to be practical in America," he comments matter-of-factly. "I am expecting to live on Social Security and the support I receive from disciples."

Mrs. Luong Nguyen is one of those disciples who support the monks at the Giac Minh temple and monastery. She attends sermons every Sunday and credits her three children's careers (in electrical engineering and medicine) to the strong moral discipline they learned at the temple. "I am grateful. My husband helped build the temple, and I cook the vegetarian food."

Minh Hoang, a social worker in San Jose with a caseload of fifty clients, says he goes to Kim Son temple in Watsonville to learn Zen meditation, to Duc Vien temple in San Jose to find solace, and to Giac Minh temple "to feel part of the community."

Mr. Linh Tran, on the other hand, comes here to pray for his mother's spirit. On the left wall in the main hall, where a twelve-foot statue of Buddha sits in serenity, are hundreds of photographs of deceased Vietnamese. Relatives like Tran come to pray for their swift journey to Nirvana.

On Vietnamese New Year (Tet) or Buddha's birthday, the temple grounds draw over two thousand, says Lloyd Pham, a devout

Buddhist and a professor at Meridian University in San Jose. "It gets so crowded that the Pentecostal church next door lets us borrow their parking lot."

I ask whether the temple has had any problems with local residents. "Everyone has been very receptive," Pham replies. "East Palo Alto has a reputation for crime but the temple reinforces the idea of peace and I think people respect that."

Outside, a young Hispanic in his late teens is about to attend church next door. I ask what he thinks of the temple. "I never went inside but I know it's the same as the church," he shrugs. "A place to go with your family on Sunday to be together and hang out."

II

On a sunny, idyllic Sunday afternoon in a neighborhood at the foot of the Los Altos Hills, in Santa Clara County, three boys are tossing a softball between them across the street from where I stand. A young man a few doors down waxes his sports car. But I'm standing in front of a Vietnamese home converted to a temple. It is a typical suburban house with a well-trimmed lawn and a two-car garage, but a visitor encounters the extraordinary the moment he opens the door.

Inside, a Vietnamese woman dressed in blue brocade is swaying in a trancelike rhythm amid smoke from incense and the urging beats of drums and cymbals and gongs. Beside her is an elaborate shrine on which stands an array of statuettes in various poses.

Every weekend this house is converted into a temple—one of a dozen *dens*, or shrines, in the Bay Area to accommodate the observance of Len Dong, an ancient Vietnamese channeling ritual that predates not only the coming of Catholic missionaries to Vietnam but also the beginnings of Buddhism, going back to a time when tribal shamans communicated directly to incorporeal beings.

"When I was young, I was skeptical," says Mrs. Que Pham, entering the room with a large tray of oranges and mangoes, "but now, in America, it's my addiction. I come to this *den* whenever I can. Our ancestors' spirits follow us to America and always grant me good luck." As a result, she claims, her jewelry business has been quite prosperous.

The dancer chosen to perform today's ceremony is a successful businesswoman herself. She owns an auto dealership.

In the Bay Area, some wealthy Vietnamese merchants flock to *dens* in homes like this one to participate in the ritual. Since their arrival in the region in the late 1970s, they have helped to revitalize the local economy with their many downtown restaurants and shops. And Len Dong, some of them claim, brings them good luck.

Practitioners of Len Dong believe that during the ritual, the dancers communicate with ancestors by inviting the spirits to enter their bodies. To begin this ceremony, Tran Hung Dao, Vietnam's most famous general—he defeated Chinese invaders in the twelfth century—has been called to enter the body of the dancer, who prances proudly on the well-worn Persian rug, holding a gleaming sword.

Facing her is a large shrine filled with fruits and colorful gifts wrapped in red cellophane paper. Above these, on three wooden shelves, stand the porcelain statuettes that represent ancient Vietnamese emperors and warriors and famous mandarins. "The large one visiting the middle is Hung Vuong," says Phan Quong, the drum player. Hung Vuong was the first Vietnamese king, around 2000 B.C.

The primary reason people come here is to communicate with their ancestors and pray for health and prosperity. "I feel uncomfortable and fear my business will face mishaps if I don't attend regularly," says one woman in her late sixties. But the *den* serves as more than a spiritual haven. In one corner of the room, two women are discussing their children's marriage prospects;

a conversation at the other end of the room is about the recent failure of a friend's business; yet another, in the kitchen, is about someone's recent demise and funeral arrangements.

Time for transformation: the spirit of General Tran Hung Dao sits majestically in his temporary body in front of the baroque shrine, and two women attendants scuttle to sit on each side of him. The spectators utter, "*Chao Ong! Chao Ong!*"—Greetings, Sire! The entranced woman whispers little instructions to the attendants—the only two who are allowed to listen to what the spirits say. And they, according to the rules of the ritual, do not disclose details of the conversation. "Such are the privileges of ancestors' attendants," says Mrs. Que Pham. "For the rest of us, it is enough to be able to observe the ancestors' presence." The general walks about, moving in a very manly manner. Then he takes a long puff on a cigarette and empties a glass of champagne while the women prepare him for new garments.

They place a red silk drape over the dancer's head. Her body trembles. When she pulls it off she stands again. One of her attendants gives her a mirror. The dancer, now in a dress more intricately embroidered than the previous blue one, gives a frosty smile, the expression of someone more bemused than benevolent. The music starts up again and she, swaying, nods approvingly at her own reflection.

Someone tells me she is now the woman warrior Trung Trac, who died fighting against the Chinese invaders in 42 A.D. with an army of women riding on elephants. The dancer reaches down to a small tray and grabs a handful of dollar bills and hands them out to the audience. She is greeted with "*Chao Co, Chao Co*"— Greetings, Lady—as the observers receive their gifts.

"You see," whispers a cheerful Mrs. Cong Nguyen, keeper of the *den*, "ancient generals and warriors love their people. They give money and grant good fortune, not take. Not corrupted like present-day generals and politicians." She gives me two dollars from the dancer. "Buy lottery tickets with this money. You have a better chance of winning."

In Vietnam, Len Dong has long been considered a backward and fatuous ritual by most members of the educated classes. Yet despite being shunned by the previous regime's intelligentsia and, until recent times, by the communist leaders, who considered it "anti-revolutionary," Len Dong thrives. It remains popular among the rural people who make up 80 percent of the Vietnamese population. Some Catholics and Buddhists partake in this national liturgy that, some claim, cleanses their souls and cures many of their maladies.

The folk ritual accompanied by gongs and drums and zither and dance—as the mediums attempt to communicate with the various spirits—harks back to a time when humans' relationship with all things seemed to have spiritual implications. "Our ritual survived for thousands of years under many wars, so communists don't affect us," says Phan Thuan with confidence. He says he is seventy-three years old and has seen four wars. "You can arrest monks and priests, but you can't arrest all the dancers in Vietnam. There won't be enough re-education camps to hold us." Then he laughs. "Besides," he says, "back in Vietnam, we bribed the Vietnamese local officers to ignore us."

Vinh Tran, a young computer programmer who has come to fetch his mother, provides this comment: "If anything, Len Dong is at least therapeutic and it provides some escapism for the older generation. These are people who did not hold power in society; so to personify powerful ancient heroes is to overcome powerlessness." For the believer, that is, a sense of community and belonging begins with establishing a place of spiritual worship, a connection to the past.

There are at least fifty *dens* in California alone, and a few as far as Virginia and Texas, according to the ceremony's informative drummer. An impressive network is said to connect Vietnamese communities in the San Diego, San Jose, Sacramento, San Francisco, and Los Angeles areas. Orange County, which has the largest Vietnamese population overseas, is said to have the most *dens*. But this ancient ritual remains for most Californians an invisible one, a private custom that takes place in homes converted to temples and stays, therefore, hidden despite all the changes its practitioners have gone through.

I lift the curtain during recess: bright light comes inside. Outside, on the sidewalk across the street, the kids are still tossing the ball back and forth in a beautiful arc under a blue sky, oblivious to swaying ancient spirits and the sounds of gongs and drumbeats that emanate from time to time from inside the house.

III

"We are descendants of Mr. Lam Quang Ty," my sister Nancy tells the group of dark-skinned old men in white pajamas. They are sitting on the cool tile floor at the entrance of the famous and colorful Holy See, better known as Cao Dai Temple, in Tay Ninh province, bordering Cambodia. "We're here to look for his grave and pay tribute," she continues.

Behind us a small film crew working for PBS records our every move. They have followed me back to Vietnam as part of the documentary *My Journey Home*.

It is Saturday and the place is packed with worshipers and, relegated to the upstairs balcony, camera-toting foreign tourists. Men and women in red, white, yellow, and blue robes stream in and out of the Holy See's vast hall. At the far end, the round, nine-foot-diameter All-Seeing Eye, the temple's sacred symbol, looks impassionately down from its pedestal at its prostrating faithful. Somewhere on the second floor, a band composed of monochord zithers, bamboo xylophones, lutes, and gongs is playing a doleful tune. There are dozens of disciples sitting around on the cool floor at the side entrance, talking and drinking tea.

Saying Great-grandfather's name out loud to them during recess is a shot in the dark. I follow my sister's declaration with a lengthy explanation as to how we are related to him and who he was. A wealthy Vietnamese living under French colonial rule in the 1930s, Great-grandfather Ty contributed money and land to the Cao Dai religion as it was being founded.

I remember that when I was a child in Saigon, I used to look at a faded black-and-white photo of him in a linen suit and hat standing next to his sleek Citroen, smiling brightly. Even when exiled to backward Tay Ninh by the French for speaking up against colonial rule, he continued to throw lavish parties that foreign dignitaries drove up from Saigon to attend. But when the French found out he'd been supporting not only the Cao Dai sect but also the underground nationalist movement, Great-grandfather fled to Siam, now Thailand, where he died. Members of the Holy See smuggled his body back to Tay Ninh province soon after for a secret burial on the rubber plantation he once owned.

In his own memoir, *The Twenty-Five Year Century*, my father recounted a rainy trip to the Tay Ninh province for his grandfather's belated funeral, going by horse cart at night in stealth, pretending to be peasants for fear of being caught by the French. Father must have been seven or eight years old. "As I clung to the corner of the seat, listening to the singsong of the small bells that danced under the horse's neck and watching the dim lights of the small petroleum lamp that swung under the roof eave of the carriage," he wrote, "I panicked at the thought of some tiger suddenly surging from the roadside bush."

That was a long, long time ago. There are no tigers left in Vietnam and much of the jungle of old has been slashed and burned. Before arriving there with Nancy on this trip, I doubted that anyone would remember Great-grandfather Ty after some seven decades. My sister and I and the film crew expect at least a day of searching for the right people, if we are lucky.

But there is a commotion among the older men the moment my great-grandfather's name is mentioned, and during the lengthy explanation, one man, in white pajamas and very dark skin, stands up rather abruptly. "We were told about your trip," he says without much fanfare, a stern face, "so we knew you were coming. Follow me."

I'm taken aback. We seem to have hit the jackpot at first try! Cao Dai's All-Seeing Eye aside, its global ear, I come to realize at that moment, is to be reckoned with. He tells us a certain Mr. Long, an old friend of our father's and a devout member of Cao Dai, has sent a letter from Los Angeles to tell temple members that we are coming.

What follows happens so fast it feels like we're all in a trance. We get into our air-conditioned van with the film crew and, under the old man's instruction, our chauffeur drives a few kilometers away from the main temple complex, passing smaller temples and hamlets until we reach a rubber plantation. The man, about sixty, gets out. He moves like a teenager, jumping over small puddles, wading through muddy patches, and climbing small knolls without pause. He treks barefoot. Dressed in simple white pajamas, he seems like an apparition among the rubber trees.

We keep going, deeper into the plantation with no apparent markers. It is quiet all around, except for the occasional bird and constant humming of cicadas. Behind my sister and me, the crew: the cameraman is from Spain, the director was born in Mexico, and the soundman hails from Brazil. They struggle to follow us while recording it all. Looking at them I am thinking how apropos it is that an international crew is following two very well-traveled Vietnamese Americans who are searching for the grave of a man who helped spur a religion that in turn embraced the entire world.

The majority of Vietnamese practice Tam Giao—or Three Religions—Buddhism, Confucianism, and Taoism. Accepting all three and making them work without too much conflict is a Vietnamese tendency and impulse. Taoism is part of our cosmology: its man-cosmos correspondence seeps into the way we cook, build our houses, take our medicine, exercise, and explain the weather. Buddhism provides solace and peace and spiritual guidance. Confucianism insures social order and familial harmony, imparts rituals, promotes filial piety within the family and clan, and emphasizes the importance of education.

But Caodaism, in comparison with Vietnam's many other religions, is a newcomer. It goes a step further than Tam Giao. Cao Dai—literally, "high tower," attempts to integrate and reconcile disparate major world religions. Graham Greene, in his classic *The Quiet American,* called Cao Dai "prophecy of planchette," as its spiritualists receive messages of wisdom from various saints through means of séance. "Christ and Buddha looking down from the roof of the Cathedral on a Walt Disney fantasia of the East," he writes, "dragons and snakes in Technicolor."

In its cosmos Cao Dai perceives Hinduism, Judaism, Zoroastrianism, Buddhism, Taoism, Confucianism, Christianity, and Islam all as human aspirations to worship and communicate with the one Supreme Being. It is why on top of the Holy See's spires there's a Buddhist swastika, a Christian cross, an Islamic crescent moon, and a Hindu Om symbol. The temple counts Moses, Joan of Arc, Louis Pasteur, Vietnamese poet and prophet Trang Trinh, Sun Yat-Sen, Victor Hugo, and Jesus among its many saints.

Great-grandfather was an acquaintance of one of Cao Dai's cofounders, Pham Cong Tac, who was a French-educated civil servant but quit his post in the French government to construct the Holy See. Great-grandfather reportedly loved the concept of integrated world religions, which is the basic tenet of Caodaism: a realization that all religions have one same origin. Cao Dai was the first Vietnamese spiritual response to globalization, long before the term existed.

We keep on trekking. Finally, there, lying at an oblique angle against the well-lined rubber trees, far from the main road, I see it: a large grave covered with lichen and surrounded by overgrown bushes. Great-grandfather's grave is the only grave in the middle of the plantation, and well hidden. That it lies at an odd angle with the trees, the old man says, "has to do with feng shui. We want to make sure his descendants do well, and he is facing this direction toward the mountain." That mountain would be Nui Ba Den— another story of Vietnamese spirituality in itself—considered the most holy mountain in the South, if not all of Vietnam.

We proceed to light incense and place flowers and fruit at the tombstone. The old man, too, prays along with us while the crew films. It is an extraordinary image: his arms raised high above his head, a bundle of joss sticks streaming and billowing smoke between bony, clutching fingers, his eyes solemn, the sunlight turning his white tunic golden.

As I stand silent in front of the lonely grave of my great-grandfather, I find kinship with him, not just through blood, but ideas. I could almost tell Great-grandfather's conflicted story: Steeped in French culture, he nevertheless wanted independence for Vietnam. He was against French rules but he otherwise embraced French styles and tastes as his own. And was it not that effort to reconcile East and West that made him support Cao Dai, a most subversive act of colonial enterprise? My story is not that different: I was French-educated as a child in Saigon, but I fled Vietnam and, despite the fact that the U.S. waged a bloody war in my homeland, embraced America wholeheartedly. Now an American writer, am I not constantly trying to find that middle path between East and West, searching and defining my place in a world where the various traditions commingle? So I, too, light incense to Great-grandfather's spirit and ask for his blessings.

———

After the documentary aired, I got this email from Professor Janet Hoskins, who teaches anthropology at the University of Southern California: "I was intrigued to see your discussion of Caodaism on the website of the PBS program *My Journey Home*," she wrote. "You might be interested to know that…there was a groundbreaking ceremony for a new Caodaist temple to be built in Garden Grove, California. Although there are about 20 small Cao Dai temples in California now, most of them are remodeled detached garages, former churches or homes, and this will be the first one to be specially built as a temple, showing the flamboyant and colorful architecture of the Great Temple at Tay Ninh which you visited."

Hoskins has been doing research on Caodaism, including fieldwork in Vietnam and Cambodia as well as visits to Cao Dai temples in Paris and vicinity. "Am documenting the rebirth of this unusual and idealistic religion in California," she wrote. There are also Cao Dai temples New Orleans, Atlanta, Maryland, Houston, and Seattle. Cao Dai centers exist in other countries, including Australia, Canada, Germany, and England.

In recent years, a number of Cao Dai leaders have begun translating their sacred texts into English and reaching out to an English-reading public. The vision of expansion goes something like this: the fall of Saigon in 1975 was part of a grander plan to send Vietnamese all over the world so that they could provide spiritual leadership, which would ultimately help members of all religions to live in harmony. It is a positive, idealistic vision for an event otherwise perceived by many Vietnamese overseas as a tragic end.

Cao Dai, so specific to Tay Ninh province, has not only revived but become a global religion, with strong footholds in America's West. I was surprised at first, but thinking of California's dynamic, highly diverse religious reality—where neighborhoods overlap one another, and where over a hundred languages are spoken and temples and mosques and synagogues are cheek by jowl—I realized that, well, Great-grandfather's syncretic religion fits right in.

IV

Graham Greene was prescient about the Vietnam War. *The Quiet American*, published at the onset of American engagement in Vietnam, was a literary divination of the horror to come. Its premise: America's anticommunist zeal, combined with its self-righteousness and inexperience, would cause more killing in Vietnam without defeating the determined, anticolonial sentiment, and the result would be catastrophe. I wouldn't be surprised if Greene were someday inducted into Cao Dai's pantheon of prophets.

Yet even Greene couldn't possibly imagine that, less than three decades after the publication of his seminal work, more than one million Vietnamese would become Americans (and, given their penchant for routinely protesting on the streets of America against communism, not so very quiet). And despite the bloody American involvement in Vietnam, despite the horror of the exodus in the aftermath, one of the astonishing outcomes of that encounter is that America's West is now dotted with Vietnamese temples, churches, and shrines.

Until 1965, when Lyndon Johnson signed into law the immigration act proposed by John F. Kennedy, U.S. immigration policy toward Asia was a policy of exclusion. But the new law changed all that, setting Asian immigration on equal footing and eliminating the quotas that had linked immigration to the national origins of groups already established in the U.S.

Chinese, Filipinos, Asian Indians, and those other Asians who already had a foothold here benefited first, gaining citizenship after years of being systematically denied that opportunity, and bringing over relatives from back home. Ten years later, in 1975, came the Vietnamese as refugees, en masse, followed by refugees from Laos and Cambodia. The rest of Southeast Asia trickled in.

Immigrants bring their own cultural practices with them—from cuisine to music to agriculture to language—but what's least explored and understood are their various religions and belief systems. The three vignettes above barely capture the ardor of Vietnamese devotion—and Vietnamese spiritual practices are but a small segment that adds to the ever-growing complexity of America's religious reality.

Yet among Vietnamese Americans lurk shamans, geomancers, and diviners as well as more traditional priests and monks. One man I met a decade ago in San Jose, California, was rumored to practice the art of necromancy. He purportedly kept jars of fetuses, and their spirits were bound to him and did his bidding. Several women I met were self-proclaimed psychics and seers who could see auras, spirits, and ghosts. Another man, a South Vietnamese vet, drew Sanskrit symbols on his patients' bodies and, while waving incense in the air, chanted mysterious mantras to cure their ailments.

In Berkeley once, I listened to a lecture by one of the most well-known Buddhists in the world, Zen master Thich Nhat Hanh. The venerable monk, who hails from Vietnam and now lives in France, has become a major influence in the development of Western Buddhism, his teachings and practices appealing to a wide swath of people from various religious and spiritual backgrounds. With nearly one hundred books on the subjects of mindfulness and meditation and "engaged Buddhism"—a form of social activism based on compassion—he attracts adherents around the globe. That evening in Berkeley his ability to communicate to Western sensibilities was amply evident when listeners practiced "tiptoe" mindfulness at the entrance of a crowded community center, straining to listen.

And I follow with both delight and wariness the story of perhaps the most conspicuous character among Vietnamese spiritual leaders in the West: a woman known as Supreme Master Ching Hai, a self-proclaimed reincarnation of both Buddha and Jesus Christ with followers spanning the globe, from Vietnam to Taiwan to California to Europe. "Ching Hai is many things: painter, poet, Buddhist nun, and spiritual leader," declared a journalist in the *Metroactive Weekly* in San Jose some years ago when she held a workshop on enlightenment at a hotel there. "She is also a fashion designer, beauty makeover consultant, and restaurateur. She also happens to own a vegetarian restaurant chain." A *Time* magazine article reported that Ching Hai wore queenly robes "under orders from God" and rode a sedan chair carried by eight bearers to the cheers of "your royal majesty." "SM" is the supreme master's monogram, sewn onto clothes she designs and sold in a catalogue to her followers. Honestly, you can't invent a character like that in fiction (though if there were one, it would seem somehow endemically Californian).

In the last half of the twentieth century, America cunningly exports itself overseas, marketing its images, ideals, and products with ingenuity and zeal, but what it has not been able to measure and imagine are the effects in the reverse. For every McDonald's or Starbucks that springs up in Taipei or Bangkok or Tokyo, a handful of Vietnamese, Chinese, and Thai restaurants bloom in the U.S. If the world is experiencing what everyone now calls the process of globalization, one based on the free exchange of information and mass migration, a large chunk of that phenomenon is shaped by the epic union between East and West.

I take it as some cosmic law of exchange that if Hong Kong and Tokyo are to have their Disneyland, then Los Angeles, home

of Hollywood and the Magic Kingdom, should be graced by
Buddhist temples. It comes as no surprise to Californians that
many scholars now agree that the most complex Buddhist city in
the world is not in Asia but in the U.S.: Los Angeles, where there
are more than three hundred Buddhist temples and centers repre-
senting nearly all of the Buddhist practices around the world.

Over the past three decades, Buddhism has become the third
most popular religion in America behind Christianity and Judaism, according to a 2008 report from the Pew Forum on Religion
and Public Life. Evidence that Buddhism is taking deep roots
in America is abundant. On CNN recently, I watched a report
on organizations working with over twenty-five hundred prison
inmates to teach them meditation and Buddha's Dharma. So successful is the program that it inspired a documentary called *The
Dhamma Brothers.*

Yet Buddhism, in its own way, and despite its message of peace
and compassion, can be a very radical spiritual practice for the
westerner, for it refutes the existence of a creator. The serious
practitioner aims to extinguish the self by defeating his own ego,
and thereby see beyond the illusion spun by the ignorant mind.
Imagine, if you will, Moses not turning his face away from the
burning bush that is God on Mount Sinai but approaching it, then
merging fully with that terrifying fire. Buddhism, notes Diana
Eck, professor of comparative religions at Harvard University,
"challenges many Americans at the very core of their thinking
about religion—at least, those of us for whom religion has something to do with one we call God."

Waves after waves of immigration have dramatically changed
and amalgamated the spiritual landscape of America, a phenomenon that is no longer relegated to the cosmopolitan coasts of
California and New York but is across the board. Muslims live
next door to Presbyterians and Zoroastrians live down the street
from Sikhs and Harikrishnans in Houston. There are Vietnamese

churches in Jackson, Mississippi, Hindu temples in Savannah, Georgia, mosques in Toledo, Ohio, Zen Buddhist temples in Detroit, Michigan, and so on.

Asia entices. Maxine Hong Kingston, author of *The Woman Warrior*, once noted that "To this day when in need of aesthetic and moral strength, American poets find it by questing eastward...Emerson, Thoreau, and Whitman reached for spiritual states that they could see in Hinduism and Buddhism. The Beats went to Japan and India and brought back modern poetry." To her list we can add Isherwood, Maugham, Huxley, and Hesse, and a horde of other important thinkers, writers, and artists. "They fantasized about us so long and so hard," she wryly concluded, "we came to them."

America may remain largely a Christian country, but the counternarratives form an epic in the making. Indeed, as ties deepen between the two continents, we are entering what many thinkers and philosophers call the second axial age, an age of pluralism in which the various spiritual traditions coexist. In the best scenario, they could come together to shape the human condition and lead humanity to an age of spiritual exploration.

In these global days, no single system can exist as a separate entity, nor can its borders remain impervious to change; all exist to various degrees of openness and exchange. The Silk Road along which so many religious ideas traveled has been replaced by a far more potent thoroughfare: the information highway, which transcends geography.

Yet hasn't that East-West dialogue always been part of America's, as old as the story of her birth? Was it not in search of Cathay and the Indies, their riches, that Columbus sailed west and instead found the continent? America's birth, in essence, was the vision of the Far East, and Native Americans were mistaken for Indians. Ever since then, that hunger for the Far East, and all of its mysteries and treasures, has endured.

In the twenty-first century the experiment in cohabitation has thus only just begun, and the American motto "e pluribus unum"—out of many, one—is currently put up for scrutiny. The challenge of pluralism is one that mutual respect should be at the core of, with mutual inquisitiveness at the periphery. Or as Professor Eck put it, "The encounter of a pluralistic society is not premised on achieving agreement, but achieving relationship." To that end, she noted, "Perhaps the most valuable thing we have in common is commitment to a society based on the give-and-take of civil dialogue at a common table."

Or argument and disagreement, as often is the case. But ours is a brave new world. While xenophobia and racism and fights over territory and ideas will always exist, increasingly people living both in the East and the West have more options than simply accepting the traditions they grew up in. It's a Tower of Babel with many prophets, but for every dozen who retreat into a comfortable homogeneous corner, there are also one or two who cross some hallway asking, "What are you about? Tell me about your beliefs. Tell me your story."

How far have we come since my arrival on this continent?

I once kept on the wall in my study two very different pictures to remind me of the way East and West have changed. One is from an article in *Time* magazine on Buddhism in America. In it, a group of American Buddhists sit serenely in lotus position on a wooden veranda in Malibu overlooking a calm Pacific Ocean. The other is of a Vietnamese American astronaut named Eugene Trinh, who made a flight on the space shuttle. The pictures tell me that East and West have not only met but also commingled and fused. When a Vietnamese man whose parents left his impoverished homeland might very well reach the moon, while Americans turn inward, breathe in and out, and try to reach inner peace and possibly Nirvana, I think that East-West dialogue has come very, very far.

LETTERS FROM A YOUNGER BROTHER

Two years before the Vietnam War ended, my older brother left
Saigon and went to live as a foreign student with our aunt and her
children in Daly City, south of San Francisco—two years, that
is, before my family and I abruptly joined him after we fled as
refugees. During that time he saved in a shoebox dozens of letters
sent by relatives and friends. The box, moved around and then
forgotten for several decades, lay hidden in a closet in my parents'
home until I found it one summer evening while helping them
throw out junk and put the house up for sale.

My parents' home fetched a handsome sum. This was before
the economy went south. A five-bedroom house in the suburbs on
the northern edge of Silicon Valley, it was their grand American
dream realized, until they grew too old to take good care of it.
Between its walls and fences the bulk of our American experience
had taken place—festive parties, weddings, funerals, barbecues,
and heartbreaking arguments—but when it went on the market
and, to our relief, closed rather quickly, there was little to do but
pose for a few pictures, then drive swiftly away.

Selling homes and moving on, after all, are endemically American, whereas running into one's distant and dissonant past is
something else altogether. Which made discovering the shoebox
full of letters not unlike, I'd imagine, what an archaeologist might
feel upon opening a sarcophagus and finding inside a mummified
version of himself.

There are letters from several writers, but chief among them are my mother, sister, and I. They are typically written on a thin blue sheet that is printed, on the other side, with a stamp; when folded it turns into a flimsy envelope. Price: 150 dong; in 1974 dollars, around 20 cents.

As I sifted through them, that profound sense of loss came back and sharpened with each passage: a way of life long gone, a loving family disrupted, a clan scattered and dispersed, and a country in ruin; grief. But above it all, I was astonished to discover someone I had thought I knew intimately—that is, until I was forced to face him again.

The round, undisciplined handwriting in Vietnamese, bordering on chaos, I instantly recognized as my own (it hasn't improved much), but the boy who wrote them was someone else—someone I scarcely knew, inaccessible not simply because of the years, but also because he hadn't crossed any borders and still spoke and dreamed in Vietnamese, his primal tongue. He was at once intimately familiar and an impossible stranger.

In fact, it took some time—months—before I found the courage to really take the plunge. No doubt I was afraid of what I would find: a version of the past that conflicted with the one that I have told and retold others and myself all these years in America.

Nov. 12, 1974: "Oy, Brother, Mom said I have to do my homework before I can write you, so it took a while. How is it over there? Uncle Phuoc said that it is like this: you can drive for kilometers and kilometers and on both sides there are trees with fruit available for the picking. Anyone can pick it. Not a problem. Correct?"

March 12, 1975: "Yoo-hoo, Brother, have you seen snow? Do you miss me? Aunt Cuc has a new dog. So very cute! I'm going to get one too, maybe in two months. It's going to be so very beautiful." This letter was written six weeks before that fateful day, April 30, 1975, when the war came to a blistering end as communist tanks came crashing through the gilded iron gate of the Independence Palace in Saigon while overhead squadrons of helicopters, carrying refugees and military personnel, flew out to awaiting U.S. Navy ships on the open sea.

"My friend told me half of your classmates are now drafted. His brother is going too!" I wrote a week later, the tone chirpy and upbeat, betraying no sense of worries, and no awareness that the war consumed young men's lives to fuel its engines. The next sentence, a non sequitur, was about my childhood obsession with stamp collecting: "I wrote to Uncle Tho in Dalat to ask for stamps. No results yet."

What could I be thinking? The war was going extraordinarily badly. Even kids younger than me knew it and talked about it at my school, and one even said he would commit suicide when the communists came into Saigon. Yet there I was, asking Uncle Tho—Father's older brother, a major general who was administrator of the Vo Bi Military Academy, one built by the Americans to reflect West Point—for stamps, when Dalat itself was under siege. A few days after I wrote that to my brother, in fact, Uncle Tho was forced to detonate the portions of the military school that held sensitive equipment, to keep it from falling into enemy hands, and then evacuate with his cadets. Many people died fleeing to Saigon, crushed by retreating tanks or slaughtered by communist mortars.

At eleven, I seemed oddly and glibly unaware of how intricately intertwined my own life was with the current events. A terrible and catastrophic epoch, like a tsunami, was about to sweep over my world, leaving in its wake lives shattered and wrecked, and I seemed to be the only one who sounded glib about it. As it turned out, not only would I not get a new dog, but the three dogs that I dearly loved, along with the house I lived in, my neighbors, relatives, schoolmates, teachers, servants, and ultimately, a way of life, would all be taken away from me as well; or to be more precise, I would be taken away from them.

The words written by everyone else pointed toward an impending doom. "Hey Bud, talk to your father if you can," my brother's high school friend begged him in a letter marked March 26, 1975. "Your father can use his influence to send me out of the country. I would be indebted to you forever." Though trying to sound casual and cool, my brother's friend could barely mask his desperation. He was, of course, being drafted.

This passage from my sister in a letter marked April 12, 1975, was as ominous as it was, if one knew her, unintentionally comical: "Cousin Phuong and I talked about how things look so bad now. If the Viet Cong come into Saigon, we will go out to the countryside, and there we'll take up arms and become guerrillas." How she could do this would be beyond imagination. The pampered teenager who refused to eat chickens from the farm outside Saigon that we owned because she'd seen them alive, and who was being chauffeured to school, then piano lessons and swimming practice at the country club called *le Cercle Sportif* didn't know how to cook and wash her own clothes, let alone use a gun and survive in the jungle. But there is no denying the seriousness of her tone, and considering the odds, its utter hopelessness.

And here, on April 2, 1975, in atypically uneven handwriting that betrays great distress, is a passage by Mother: "The situation is chaotic. I hope that because we have been good people we will manage to escape this dire situation. But no matter what, listen to me carefully: *Don't come home!* Even if later you get a letter from me, or your father, do not believe it. Love you very much. Mother."

Father, who had just barely survived the evacuation of Da Nang, and who had just come back to Saigon the day before, managed to write a succinct paragraph in a letter with three stars as its letterhead to say the same thing. "I'm safe. No matter what, continue your education. If we ever tell you to come home, you are to stay put and continue your studies. Stay in America!" Both my parents were afraid that after the war ended, they would be forced by the communist rulers to send for their eldest son—the only one who got away.

Yet in a letter dated March 30, 1975, when we still did not know for sure if Father would make it back alive from Da Nang, I, upon learning that my brother now worked in a supermarket, wrote: "Be careful stacking eggs and don't break them! *The Exorcist* is about to be shown here. Oh, how scary! Good-bye."

Good-bye indeed. For that was the last letter I wrote from Vietnam, and most likely the last letter I ever wrote in Vietnamese. Not too many people have their childhood end so precisely on a historical marker, such as the end of a catastrophic war, and then subsequently are sent into exile, but that was what happened to me. The war ended. We fled. And I quickly transformed into someone else entirely.

When I came to America I suffered a kind of self-imposed amnesia. A few months after my arrival, my voice broke. A rasp quickly replaced the lilt, and I went from a child speaking Vietnamese to a craggy-sounding teenager speaking broken English.

When I replied in Vietnamese to a teacher's question that first day in school, the entire class erupted in jeers and laughter. I remember feeling terrible shame. I desperately embraced English so I wouldn't stand out. Each morning, each night, I practiced new vocabulary words out loud. I mimicked characters from sitcoms and memorized entire TV commercials, reciting jingles like mantras. I devoured novels. I sang American Top Forty tunes.

Trouble was, in our home speaking English was a no-no. And my parents constantly scolded me.

Then one day my brother said, with a serious voice, "Mom and Dad told you not to speak English all the time, and you didn't listen. Now look what happened. You shattered your vocal cords. That is why you sound like a duck."

Since no one had bothered to tell me about the birds and the bees, I fully believed him. I was duped for what seemed like a long, long time, until a friend told me in very graphic terms what puberty entails.

But I also remember being of two minds: as I mourned the loss of my homeland, I also marveled at how speaking a new language could change me. I was at an age when magic and reality still share a porous border, and speaking English was like chanting magical incantations. My new language was reshaping me from inside out. Did it not alter my vocal cords, change my body, my outlook?

It was also the first time that I paid attention to my own voice. I heard myself, the way I sounded, observed the effects my words had on others. So much so that by the time I went to high school a few years later, I had stopped speaking Vietnamese altogether, had more or less shaved the Vietnamese accent from my new tongue, and, at times, pretended that I was American-born. I even changed my Vietnamese name to an American one.

Left behind to cobweb and dust was the boy with a Vietnamese name who sat writing these letters, dreaming of adventures in fabled America, its 31-flavors ice cream, its majestic mountains and endless orchards, its impossibly tall high-rises and multi-tiered freeways, its falling snow.

For years in America the story I often told others was the one in which I was a precocious child—an imaginative bookworm who learned to play Chinese chess at four and was a fan of Victor Hugo and Chinese epics, someone whose worldly-wise father and upper-class background imbued him with a cultivated sheen. The implication was that the transition to America was smooth, a natural trajectory. But memories are a tricky business. If I took pride in having impeccable memories of events in Vietnam, in being one of those few boys who read newspapers at eight and, rarer still, who got to see the war from their father's chopper, the truth was that, as an American adult, I could barely conceive of the emotional life of that boy who went through an extraordinary time in that ill-fated country at the southeast end of Asia.

Going over the letters, I was transported back to a childhood that was somehow sacred and yet all but faded. Reading, for example, this passage out loud in Vietnamese—*Be careful stacking eggs and don't break them! The Exorcist is about to be shown here. Oh, how scary!*—I saw an afternoon long lost. I had wanted to go see that very scary movie that caused people to faint, but considering the tense situation at the time, and the subject matter, my mother strictly forbade it, and I sulked.

I did not remember that Aunt Cuc had a new dog but upon reading *that* passage I saw her as a pretty newlywed who was busy making her new home with my uncle, my mother's youngest brother, who was a pilot in the Vietnamese Air Force, and in whose living room sat an enormous fish tank populated with lionhead goldfish that drifted to and fro and kept me and my cousins enthralled on a few lazy afternoons while our mothers visited our maternal grandmother, who lived with another uncle and his very large family next door.

I did not remember Father's letterhead, either, but I recognized it immediately, having played at his desk at the military base in Hue, and in reading his succinct paragraph I remembered, too, the evening when Mother sat with Father's best friend, a powerful, well-connected woman whose husband was a colonel, whom we called *Tata* Toan. She and Mother were planning to rescue Father and Uncle Tho and five other generals who had all been jailed in a trailer park in the military headquarters near the Tan Son Nhat Airport after they retreated from South Vietnam's four heavily guarded regions to protect Saigon. President Thieu had ordered the retreat, but upon their return he also ordered their arrest, for fear of a military coup. The rescue did not happen. After Thieu fled the country with his entourage a week before the war ended, Defense Minister Tran Van Don signed papers to release Father and Uncle Tho and the other generals. But by then their army had fallen apart, scattered, soldiers changing into civilian clothes, throwing away their M-16s. My father boarded a naval ship and headed for the open sea when news came that communist tanks had crashed through the iron gates of the Independence Palace and Saigon had fallen, but that, as they say, is another story.

I read out loud some more. Ordinary moments captured in time were now full of mystery. *Have you seen snow? Do you miss me?* I saw a long-forgotten image: a boy on a chair with his hands in the freezer compartment, scraping and scraping at the frost until his fingers were numbed but his eyes stared dreamily at the modest snowball in his palm. What was he thinking? Was he trying to commune with his worldly brother?

I heard his voice, perhaps for the first time. Along with it, the old life once more revealed itself to me—family and clan, the feeling of being insulated in my primal language that once held everyone I knew within its familial insularities, a walled garden.

It all came back. A courtyard drenched in sunlight; three dogs asleep in the doorway; and above the rusting iron gates, red bougainvillea wavering, shading blue sky. A little boy sat at his desk reading, and above that desk were his treasures: *Tintin*, *Spirou*, and *Asterix et Obelix* comic books, and Chinese martial arts novels, and of course an extensive stamp collection. Then the street vendor's lyrical voice echoed abruptly in the quiet afternoon—*Ai an bong co hot luu khong?*—"Who wants grass jelly and passion fruit soup?"—and her voice, with its sorrowful resonance, pierced his soul.

And those unsettling nights near the end of the war...Cool spring breezes that carried the deep and rhythmic sounds of exploding bombs from the faraway countryside through the open windows and, along with the chirps of insects and the croaks of frogs, sounded like some strange lullaby. *Ka-booom...ka-boom... ka-boom...*And how, listening to Mother's muffled cries in the next room, the boy, too, wept into his pillow as he struggled toward sleep...

Then early one bleak morning, he was on a cargo plane full of crowded refugees, and the war, its people, and a beloved country—a way of life—turned into a vast green sea...

———

When I speak Vietnamese now, I speak it as someone who left his homeland as a child speaks it. Informed by the many-layered memories and far-flung particularities of a multilingual immigrant, my expressions are adulterated by English vocabulary, my voice inflected with a Californian accent, which is to say, slightly optimistic. I do not speak Vietnamese the way my parents speak it: as insiders, full of eloquence and Vietnamese cultural and historical references and, therefore, melancholy.

Perhaps this is why, though I have spoken about the war and my Vietnamese childhood, I have found it difficult to write in depth about it in English. While I could easily write about my Americanization process, to examine my Vietnamese childhood in English has seemed at times nearly impossible. Or rather, because I used English to construct my new self, that language somehow became incapable of reaching the boy who once dreamed in his mother tongue, who wandered in his mother's garden.

But I am the keeper of my brother's letters now. From time to time I take them out of their leather-bound folder and read them the way one reads psalms. The past is gone, but the past is ever-present; I take comfort in seeing those thin pages in which our family left no space unfilled. Written to a faraway brother, the letters now address me. They tell me that it is easy to forget all the sadness, all the fear and joy, forget who we used to be, and how we used to feel. Yet they also confirm that those very emotions—the wishes, yearnings, and hope—are not lost but, in various ways, still operating in me.

And it is only now, after so many years have passed and I have made an accounting of my losses and gains; only now, with the knowledge that love, written in any language, can transcend time and space, that I begin to believe and trust that my stepmother tongue could intimate the cadence of the heart and thereby commune between the hemispheres.

———

Brother, have you seen snow?

So much that it blinds in the recall, little one. Falling on the Ponte di Rialto in Venice, covering the rock gardens and temple rooftops of fabled Kyoto, blanketing the Himalayas, and drifting across the great American plains.

In Lake Tahoe some years ago, while skiing with a few friends, I got lost when I went down the side of a mountain where I could see no one around. Snow covered the landscape before me—mountains, trees, rocks, ravines, all under a gray sky. There was so much beauty in that void, a blank page; there was I, alone. To say I panicked would be understating it. Before I knew it, I heard myself sing out that old song you sang at school during recess in Dalat. *Gap nhau day roi chia tay*…"We meet today then we say good-bye but such is life." So goes its first line. "Through rivers and mountains, let's reunite tomorrow." So goes the last.

But I didn't remember all the words in between and had to make up the rest with French and English thrown in, as if somehow the words, strung together and sung, could connect me from where I was to where I am and where I am going.

I think about that moment now, where neither East nor West existed in that vast solitude, and all I had was an unsteady voice and a fragmented song, like a strange new prayer, to keep me calm. Little one, you would be proud to know that I kept on singing, forming new words on my tongue—I kept at it until I saw movement in the distance and found my bearings at last and trudged off on my way toward civilization.

ABOUT THE AUTHOR

Andrew is an editor and cofounder of New America Media, an association of over two thousand ethnic media outlets in America. His essays have appeared in dozens of newspapers and magazines across the country, and his short stories are anthologized widely. A three-time winner of the Society of Professional Journalists Award, Lam was also the recipient of the Rockefeller Fellowship at UCLA and the John S. Knight Fellowship at Stanford. He was featured in the documentary *My Journey Home*, in which a film crew followed him back to his homeland, Vietnam, and which aired on PBS nationwide in 2004. He has been a regular commentator on NPR's *All Things Considered*.

His book *Perfume Dreams: Reflections on the Vietnamese Diaspora* won a PEN American Beyond Margins Award in 2006 and was a finalist for the Asian American Literary Award. Lam's first short story collection, *Birds of Paradise*, is due in 2011. He is working on a novel.

HEYDAY
into California

About Heyday

Heyday is an independent, nonprofit publisher and unique cultural institution. We promote widespread awareness and celebration of California's many cultures, landscapes, and boundary-breaking ideas. Through our well-crafted books, public events, and innovative outreach programs we are building a vibrant community of readers, writers, and thinkers.

Thank You

It takes the collective effort of many to create a thriving literary culture. We are thankful to all the thoughtful people we have the privilege to engage with. Cheers to our writers, artists, editors, storytellers, designers, printers, bookstores, critics, cultural organizations, readers, and book lovers everywhere!

We are especially grateful for the generous funding we've received for our publications and programs during the past year from foundations and hundreds of individual donors. Major supporters include:

Anonymous; Audubon California; Barona Band of Mission Indians; B.C.W. Trust III; S. D. Bechtel, Jr. Foundation; Barbara and Fred Berensmeier; Berkeley Civic Arts Program and Civic Arts Commission; Joan Berman; Lewis and Sheana Butler; Butler Koshland Fund; California State Coastal Conservancy; California State Library; California Wildlife Foundation; Joanne Campbell; Keith Campbell Foundation; Candelaria Fund; John and Nancy Cassidy Family Foundation, through Silicon Valley Community Foundation; Christensen Fund; Creative Work Fund; The Community Action Fund; Community Futures Collective; Compton Foundation, Inc.; Lawrence Crooks; Ida Rae Egli; Donald and Janice Elliott, in honor of David Elliott, through Silicon Valley Community Foundation; Evergreen Foundation; Federated Indians of Graton Rancheria; Mark and Tracy Ferron; Furthur Foundation; George Gamble; Wallace Alexander Gerbode Foundation; Richard & Rhoda Goldman Fund; Evelyn & Walter Haas, Jr. Fund; Walter & Elise Haas Fund; James and Coke Hallowell; Sandra and Chuck Hobson; James Irvine Foundation; JiJi Foundation; Marty and Pamela Krasney; Robert and Karen Kustel, in honor of Bruce Kelley; Guy Lampard and Suzanne Badenhoop; LEF Foundation; Michael McCone; Moore Family Foundation; National Endowment for the Arts; National Park Service; Organize Training Center; David and Lucile Packard Foundation; Patagonia; Pease Family Fund, in honor of Bruce Kelley; Resources Legacy Fund; Alan Rosenus; Rosie the Riveter/WWII Home Front NHP; San Francisco Foundation; San Manuel Band of Mission Indians; Deborah Sanchez; Savory Thymes; Hans Schoepflin; Contee and Maggie Seely; James B. Swinerton; Swinerton Family Fund; Taproot Foundation; Thendara Foundation; TomKat Charitable Trust; Lisa Van Cleef and Mark Gunson; Marion Weber; John Wiley & Sons; Peter Booth Wiley; and Yocha Dehe Wintun Nation.

Getting Involved

To learn more about our ┌ 3 1901 04979 4201 ┐ ther ways you can participate, please visit: www.heydaybooks.com.